In *The Making of a BraveHearted Woman* Dawn takes readers through the what, when, why and how to get out of the victim mentality to be God-given women of courage and purpose. If you're ready to be strong, brave, bold and beautiful full of self confidence and self esteem to be a better wife, mother, daughter, sister, aunt, grandmother, coworker, boss, and/or friend, to fulfill make your God-sized dreams a reality, this book is for you!"

Brea Sharron Estep
Integrative Health Practitioner
Mrs. United States 2021-2022
www.breasharron.com

Creative. Compelling. Captivating. Courageous. These words describe Dawn Damon's powerful book, *The Making of a Brave Hearted Woman*. If you're in the second half of life and feel like you might have run out of options for a productive and purposeful life, read this book. This poignant masterpiece will give you step-by-step instructions that will lead to significant, Christ-centered transformation."

Carol Kent, Founder & Executive
Director of Speak Up Ministries
Speaker and Author, *Becoming a Woman of Influence*

Ladies, if you are ready to transform your midlife into a remarkable journey of unstoppable courage and confidence then Dawn Damon's *The Making of a BraveHearted Woman* is for you! With the voice of a BraveHearted trailblazer, Dawn Damon inspires women to step into their own courage with purpose and unshakeable confidence. Get this book!

Sam Sorbo, Education Freedom Advocate,
Award-winning Filmmaker, Best-selling Author.
SamSorbo.com

THE MAKING OF A

BRAVE *Hearted* WOMAN

COURAGE
CONFIDENCE
& VISION
IN MIDLIFE

DAWN DAMON

The Making of a Brave *Hearted* Woman

Courage, Confidence, and Vision in Midlife

DAWN DAMON

Bold Vision Books
PO Box 2011
Friendswood, TX 77546

Copyright ©Dawn Damon 2023

ISBN 978-1-962705-01-1
Library of Congress Control Number 2023948057

All rights reserved.
Published by Bold Vision Books, PO Box 2011,
Friendswood, Texas 77549   www.boldvisionbooks.com

Cover Design by Barefaced Media
Interior design by *k*ae Creative Solutions
Edited by Karen Porter
Published in the United States of America.

All rights reserved. No part of this publication may be reproduced, stored in a retrieval system, or transmitted in any form or by any means—electronic, mechanical, photocopy, recording, or any other—except for brief quotations in printed reviews, without the prior permission of the publisher.
Bible versions used are noted on page 189

Dedication

This book is dedicated to all the BraveHearted Women who have made an impact on my life. Thank you. And to my three daughters, seven granddaughters, and great-granddaughter. I pray I have taught you to be bravehearted women and confident daughters of the Lord Most High. This is the legacy I give to you and trust you will give to your daughters and granddaughters.

Table of Contents

Part 1: Brave Beginnings

Chapter One

Fire Up Your Brave: Get Ready to Shine

Set your life on fire. Seek those who fan your flames.

—Rumi

Since you're reading this book, I'm going to assume you're not interested in living average. You want more, a life filled with fire, passion, and fullness. You want to live with the windows wide open, wind in your face, on the road to destiny. Or at least you *want* to want that.

So did LouAnn.

LouAnn's Story

LouAnn plopped down on the couch, stuffed a pillow behind her back, and propped her feet on the coffee table without missing a beat. Her Starbucks mocha latte was still pressed against her lips as she slurped the hot, frothy pick-me-up.

"Well, I made it through another month," she mused.

LouAnn, a woman in her late 50s, just arrived for another coaching appointment. I enjoyed our conversations, but I wondered how valuable these meetings were. Month after month, LouAnn bemoaned her circumstances. I understood why: her body was out of shape and overweight, the career she once excelled in had ended, and her elderly father needed nursing care. Her youngest daughter was angry and wouldn't speak to her, she was bored in her marriage, and she needed a knee replacement because the extra 75 pounds she carried had finally taken its toll. In a phrase, she was *out of shape*—physically, mentally, and spiritually.

"I'm glad you made it. Tell me some good news! How have you done on your goals this month?" I started in with my usual energetic but sincere pep talk.

"Not great. I've been so tired lately, and exercising with my knee pain is hard. I get discouraged when I eat all the right foods and still gain weight. Plus, I babysat my son's cats this month, which took more work than anticipated. I may be allergic to them. I've been wheezing all week. I didn't get a chance to update my resume' because my computer died. I don't know. I'm not very good with technology. It just feels like everything is so doggone difficult. I can't keep up like I used to. I read some this month, so that's good." She sighed and added, "I guess."

I nodded to show I was listening. Paused. Nodded again, trying to conceal my agitation. I knew LouAnn needed a breakthrough. It was time I took a different approach.

"Yes, you've been up against some challenges. But LouAnn, I'm going to probe here. You may not like me when we're done, but you didn't hire me so you could stay stuck. You hired me so you could make changes in your life. And so far, you're making more excuses than progress. Why don't we talk about what's really going on? You said life is hard. Sure, it is, but hard is a part of life, and you will have it either now or later.

Let me explain:

Hard now is disciplining your eating habits and saying no to some treats you want to nibble on. But hard later is having more surgeries because your body is breaking down. Hard now is writing a resume' and sending it to prospects, but hard later is working a job you hate because you desperately need the money and can't afford to be selective. Hard now is setting the alarm to wake up early so you can exercise, pray, and read your Bible. Hard later is being too feeble to walk up a flight of stairs or get on the floor to play with your grandkids. LouAnn, you get to choose your *hard*."

I continued.

"Frankly, I don't think you're afraid to do hard things. You're a strong woman. You've been an educator and held great jobs in corporate America. But, LouAnn, I think you have something else going on. Let's see if we can explore a bit. Tell me, what is your vision for your future? Where do you see yourself in 1, 3, or 5 years?"

LouAnn searched my face for the answers. I stared back as if to say, "I can't help you on this one." Soon her countenance dropped, her head shaking back and forth.

"I don't know. That's the problem. I see nothing. It's all a blank, bleak canvas. I've lost my confidence, and I can't picture one month from now, let alone one year. I've lost my relevance, and my skills are antiquated. I've let my body go, and I can't seem to get back in the zone. Honestly, Coach, my life needs a complete overhaul, and I'm, well, I'm so afraid! What if this is all there is for me? I don't dare to try, only to end up a failure."

There it was. LouAnn had no vision. She could not re-imagine herself living a purposeful second half of life.

She was terrified to believe for something great and worthwhile, only to fall short. Her fear of dreaming of a beautiful future kept her chained to an average life. Fearful, visionless, and without hope, LouAnn was stuck.

Being brave isn't the absence of fear. Being brave is having that fear but finding a way through it.

—Bear Grylls

LouAnn is not an anomaly. Hundreds of thousands of women share similar sentiments. They're in a crisis of vision, unable to envision a future for themselves. They don't believe a thrilling, fulfilling next chapter is waiting ahead. But they desperately want one.

Perhaps that's you.

Have you surrendered to fear? Believing your best days are behind you? Will you remain a hostage to "possibility blindness," living without a dream?

Read on, but be aware.

This book is not for the faint of heart, or better said, for those who want to **stay** faint of heart. This guide is for those who want to become brave! I'm writing for the woman with a flicker of hope, ready to wage war with mediocrity. You, who know you don't want a bland life of boredom. Misery. Or, worse, invisibility.

This book is written with you in mind.

And here is the first principle I want you to understand. Your life can change. You can start a new life for yourself at any moment and in an instant. It all starts with one decision.

Just one. *I've had enough.*

Change begins when you decide you're ready for change—ready for more.

Jim Rohn said it well, *"You can't change your destiny overnight but you can change your direction overnight."*

When you make that quality choice, a shift begins—not only in the realm of the divine unseen, because all of heaven agrees with you, but a shift in your mindset. This disruptive shift interferes with automatic thinking patterns called neuro-pathways. Now, your brain can absorb new information and write a new script.

This shift of mind, my sister-friend, is where the most significant change must occur. Once you decide you've had enough of your old way of life and you're desperate to transform, your former programming will not give you the life you want. Old pathways cannot deliver you to new destinations.

So, that's where we start—with you giving your best yes to change. Then, as the inside life reorganizes and renews, the outside life will follow.

Say Yes to the Decision

Yes, I'm ready to fire up my brave and change my life. I choose hard now.

If you've made that decision, this guide will radically transform you and your life. Together, we will unlock the secrets to experiencing a rich and satisfying life; a life where you're living your dreams, using your gifts, serving and contributing to the world, and making an impact.

If you're not sure you're ready for this bold, brave living, ask yourself these questions;

◊   If I do nothing to change or grow, how will next year look different?

◊   If next year, I'm still in the same place (or worse, because nothing stays the same), will I be fulfilled?

◊   If the answer is no, when will I be ready to face my situation and make changes?

◊   Finally, how much will losing another year of my life cost me?

Don't lose another year of your precious, one and only life.

Because on the other side of this vision crisis is another *you*. She's waiting for you and cheering you on. I'll introduce her to you soon.

Or you can pass and stay the same.

Which version of *you* do you want to live out the rest of your days?

Exactly.

The best one.

So, let's get started!

Author's Note

Throughout this book, as I refer to the *true self, self-confidence, self-discipline*, and other uses, I am not talking about the **self**-life of the old nature, as if we can somehow improve the fallen nature of humanity on our own. Absolutely not.

I believe in the crucified life—putting to death the old nature and "putting on" the new.

I'm talking about the personal life of our humanity, taking the life God has given us and becoming fully developed in our personhood. Not apart from Christ, but according to his power that is at work in us. (See Ephesians 3:20).

The parable of Luke 19 tells the story of a certain nobleman (a picture of Christ) who entrusted ten servants with his money, asking them to do business and invest wisely while he was away. When the nobleman returned, the servants had to give an account. We only read of the outcomes of three of the servants. Two invested the money given to them and received a reward. But the third servant covered and hid what the master entrusted to him out of fear, believing the nobleman was harsh and unloving.

It's what we often do. We hide and layer up what God gives us because we don't fully trust in the love of God. Instead, we follow religious constructs, assuming these will renew our shadow side and cause us to grow and develop.

When reading Peter Scazzero's book, *Emotionally Healthy Spirituality: It's Impossible to Be Spiritually Mature, While Remaining Emotionally Immature,* I saw in the endnotes an attribution to M. Robert Mulholland, which says it well, *"Self is used here not in the contemporary sense of the psychological 'self,' an implicitly reductionistic term, but in the larger biblical sense of personhood framed within the context of a life lived in relationship with God, in community with others, and as part of creation."* [1]

We cannot perfume and improve the sinful carnal nature to enough goodness that we make it into heaven.

That reality, however, does not excuse us from growing, evolving, and living fully engaged, emotionally rich and healthy, intellectually alive, and physically and financially vibrant.

Chapter Two

Where Brave Hearts are Born:
The Essence of Brave

Life is either a daring adventure or nothing.

—Helen Keller

I made a discovery at 46 years of age.

My life careened out of control and tossed me to a fork in the road. Wounded by betrayal, I lay in the rubble of a shattered life—nothing to return to. Everything I knew and loved was gone. Obliterated. That my husband of 28 years could choose to leave me—and our family—and merrily float down the jolly path of a new life while I was smoldering in a heap of ashes left me stunned and grief-stricken. My marriage, family, pastoral career, and livelihood billowed up in smoke. I despaired to the depths of my soul, devolving into a frightened, huddled mass. The only time in my life I was more afraid was when my 10-year-old daughter was fighting for her life after being struck by a car. Now, I was fighting for my life. Broadsided and left for dead, feeling fearful and alone. With the formidable crossroad ahead, I didn't know how to go on. *What am I going to do? How will I survive? Who's going to take care of me? Who am I, if not a wife, a pastor, a counselor?*

Until this moment, I had never lived a day of life alone.

My path was a common one. Childhood home, a semester at the local college, and on to the security of married life. I was never independent of another human in nearly five decades of living.

For months I sorrowed losing the life I once knew and loved. Honestly, my marriage wasn't pure bliss—far from it. Infidelity and financial reversals plagued us, but I turned a blind eye by claiming forgiveness. It was a hot mess for sure, but it was my safe and secure mess. I needed my role as a wife-martyr.

But now, whether or not I liked it (and I didn't like it one bit,) I was forced into this unwelcomed adventure, similar to my kids at the famous theme park, Cedar Point. My three children were terrified of the rollercoasters and refused to ride them. After wandering around the park for an hour, we rallied for a family meeting. We firmly told the three teary-eyed, wilted cotton candy-holding children, "You will ride these rollercoasters. You will have fun. And you will like it. Got it?" It was the classic parent pep-talk.

Now, I needed the pep talk. It was time to get myself together. *Dawn, you have to press on. You have to heal, recover, and pick yourself back up. You can't stay curled up in this ball of fear and regret. You will ride this ride, and with God's help, you will enjoy life again. Girl, you have to rise. It's time to become BRAVE.* I washed my tear-stained face and decided to take it one day at a time. I'd try my best at courage.

Brave didn't show up every morning. Some days, I lacked the willpower to get out of bed. On those days, I pulled the covers over my head and allowed myself a good cry. But eventually, a tiny brush of hope arrived with the morning. God's new mercy—bringing me enough inspiration to face the day without melting into a puddle of pain. And at night, the loneliest minutes of every single day, I squeaked out an earnest prayer, "God, thank you for getting me through this day. Please help me sleep and please give me strength for tomorrow."

Courage doesn't always roar. Sometimes courage is the little voice at the end of the day that says I'll try again tomorrow.

—Mary Anne Radmacher

Bravery didn't always roar. Some days, it barely peeped. But I was finding my new voice, squeaky as it was. Finally, at 46 years old, my brave heart was born. Through the fire, I discovered her—my true self. She was brave, and I liked her.

Brave on the Horizon

I remember the day a slice of sunshine entered my soul. For months, I chose courage as a conscious, daily decision. (Remember my classic pep-talk. You will ride this ride?) But on this spring morning in 2008, brave chose me. Courage awakened my heart and beamed into my darkened soul.

With my wounds mostly healed, I aimed toward midlife reinvention. It was a small beginning, but exhilarating because becoming a withering, frail, wounded, bitter woman hadn't been on my bucket list. Now, a brand new me was ready to try out my new wings.

I'm not the only one with brave on the horizon.

If you're a midlife woman reading this book, you know you also face reinvention. It may be at your choosing, or like me, you may be on a forced adventure. If so, I am praying for you, dear reader. But either way, midlife brings us all to the crossroads of transition—the closing chapter of the first half of life and the opening of the next. If clarity and vision for your future fill your heart, congratulations! You're a woman positioned to crush the second half of life. But, if you fear that the next chapter of your life's storyline will be a boring read and your only adventure will be trips down memory lane, I invite you to slam shut that old book and open up a brand-new one. A more authentic version of yourself is waiting up ahead.

There is freedom waiting for you, On the breezes of the sky.
And you ask, "What if I fall?"

Oh, but my darling,

What if you fly?

—Erin Hanson

The Grit and Glitter of Brave

BRAVE- *Ready to endure or face danger, pain, or unpleasant conditions while still showing courage.*

Let's explore what it means for you to be brave and what it means to become a bravehearted woman.

Throughout the centuries, brilliant minds have pondered what it means to be brave.

To Aristotle, bravery was a virtue.

To Nelson Mandela, bravery meant conquering fear, even when you feel afraid.

To Brene' Brown, bravery is risking vulnerability.

To scientists, bravery is a heroic act. (The amygdala on overdrive, acting without logic or reason, coming from the brain's fight-or-flight response center.)

To Jeff Wise, science author, bravery is:

In biological terms, bravery emerges from a primal struggle between the brain's decision-making hub, the prefrontal cortex, and the focal point of fear: the amygdala. When we find ourselves in an unexpected and dangerous situation, the amygdala sends a signal to the prefrontal cortex that interferes with our ability to reason clearly. [2]

To me, bravery is of the heart. It's the inner courage, fortitude, grit, and guts required to unleash yourself in authenticity and boldly stand in your truth, living from your heart. Brave is what it takes to look yourself in the mirror every morning and say, "Girl, you got this!" Through the essence of brave-heartedness, we raise ourselves out of mediocrity and connect with our deepest, boldest, most profound vision. We leave the place of fear and scarcity and step into a life overflowing in fullness. We dream our dream, and then we live it.

Simply put, living as a bravehearted midlife woman takes grit and … glitter!

The easy path into the future is undoubtedly to hang up our heels and retire our badge. But retiring from a fully engaged life is a subtle and insidious shift to invisibility. "Let the young women take their turn now," we say as we excuse ourselves from center stage. But here's the opportunity to encourage you. It's both of our turns. Help the young women find their way, but stay as the leading lady in your story, not a background actor. You're the star of your show.

Remember when we were young women? How we needed the courage to learn the mysteries of life. We were adulting, growing in character, patience, and maturity.

We braved the world, learning from experience and trial and error. Some of us had wonderful mentors. As we matured, we learned not to take disappointments personally, to lace our words with gentleness, and to hone our skills and abilities. As a result, many of us found our voice and our power. We learned to embrace ourselves and accept our flaws.

We discovered confidence made us sexy, and we learned how to unbridle ourselves in times of intimacy with our spouse. We learned to pray. To fight. To bloom and become.

And then, just as we had ourselves *mostly* figured out, life changed. Right? One day we looked into the mirror, and there we saw our mother staring back. *When did I become my mom?* Our youth bid us *adieu*.

Now you and I need a new courage, a new brave.

The courage it takes to make essential changes and stay fully engaged in life when you'd rather drift into obscurity. The courage nudging you to keep going when exhaustion creeps over your soul, telling you to relax, rest, chill, "You've done your part. You can take the easy road now." You need the fortitude to resist the useless prattle, for if you listen to the whispers of a weary amygdala, you will relinquish the most significant moment of life—to live in this world as a wise woman like a seasoned and beautifully aged wine. A woman of depth. Forged in the fire. Refined by trials and made into gold. A woman who has everything to offer.

Bravehearted woman, you are a glittering gem. A diamond to shine. And this is your finest hour.

> *I'm not funny. I'm brave.*
> —Lucille Ball

Brave's Anatomy

When brave hearts are born, three elements are present:

◊ Resilience

◊ Truth-Telling

◊ Courageous Action

I call these three the anatomy of brave. And although other qualities of brave exist, they almost always flow out of one of the three virtues we must possess.

Resilience

Resilience says, *I won't quit. Not on myself or my dreams.* In the chapters ahead, I'll teach you how to stay so passionate about life you'll wake up with excitement and plenty of resilience for each new day.

Not only are mental toughness and determination ingredients of resilience, but also included in resilience is the idea of the ability to recover quickly from adverse circumstances and events. How fast you can get back up on your stilettos after falling speaks to your resilience. A resilient person bounces back after perceived failures, criticisms, disappointments, financial setbacks, betrayals, and rejections. If it's a brave heart you're after, and I trust it is, then bravery demands, you get back up, brush yourself off, and stay committed to living your best life after you feel your hurt and honor yourself by acknowledging you've taken a blow.

I often teach my clients how to overcome what I've coined the A-Trap. Seven A-words that will attack your resilience and drain the stick-to-it-ness right out of you. I share them here so you can survey your heart. Are any of these draining your resilience?

The A-Trap

- Aimlessness—Having no direction, goal, or plan.

- Anxiety—Feeling worried, uneasy, and fearful.

- Ambivalence—Torn between two contradictory desires or ideas simultaneously.

- Apathy—Lacking interest, concern, or enthusiasm.

- Atrophy—Gradual decline in effectiveness or vitality due to neglect.

- Aloneness—Experiencing isolation, friendlessness, or loneliness.

- Avoidance—Practicing withdrawal, escape, or procrastination.

The A-Trap lies in wait, to capture your midlife heart and mind, draining the joy of living. If you identify one of these areas has a grip on you, I encourage you to tell a trusted and praying confidant. Jesus wants you free.

Truth-Telling

The second element in the anatomy of brave is truth-telling.

Someone once said, "Bravery is not the courage to face your enemy, but the courage to tell your friend the truth." I believe those words. It's difficult to give people we love tough feedback. But let's go one step further—bravery is the courage to face yourself in the mirror and tell yourself the truth. Not a watered-down or fluffy version of what we wish were true, nor a performance filled with explanations and excuses. But a genuine, clear-eyed self-awareness of yourself, your actions, and your circumstances.

As bravehearted women, we own enough confidence and self-esteem to relish the truth and consider reality as our friend. We don't shrink in defeat when facing hard facts or avoid self-reflection altogether. Instead, we bravely rise and declare by faith our authority to grow, change, reach, and endure.

Here's what I mean; in Romans 4:19, the Scripture talks about Abraham, the father of our faith, as a man waiting for God to fulfill what God had promised him. The verse says, "Without weakening in his faith, he faced the fact that his body was as good as dead—since he was about a hundred years old—and that Sarah's womb was also dead" (NIV).

Did you catch that? Without weakening in his faith, he faced the facts. That's the brave I'm talking about. Truth-telling doesn't mean acquiescing to circumstances. Not at all. It means we honestly evaluate our current situation—not denying the existence of facts but denying their right to override our faith. The highest truth is what God says. The

God who "gives life to the dead and calls those things which do not exist as though they did" (Romans 4:17 NIV).

> *Courage doesn't happen when you have all the answers. It happens when you are ready to face the questions you have been avoiding your whole life.*
>
> —Shannon L. Alder

Actions

Without action, brave does not exist.

Life rewards action. As a bravehearted woman, you've learned to make moves and take smart risks. For what is bravery if not heroic action?

Teacher and author Joyce Meyers says when facing difficult things, "Just do it afraid." Despite fear, a bravehearted woman acts and takes steps of faith. Think about it: if fear doesn't exist, bravery isn't required. Being brave assumes there are fearful conditions surrounding you. These fears cause you to employ the three elements of —resilience, truth-telling, and action. These all must work together in the constant presence of fear.

◊   "I feel afraid, but I won't quit." Here, bravery takes a stand as resilience.

◊   "I feel fear, but I accept responsibility." Here, bravery is truth-telling.

◊   "I feel afraid, but I will ..." Here, bravery dresses up as determined action.

If we waited to act on significant matters until we felt no fear, we'd stall out. But because life rewards action—not indecision or procrastination, not ambivalence or cowardice—brave heartedness compels us to face the fear and do it anyway. So, we lay comfort and convenience on the line and take the risk of moving forward. To me, even baby steps are heroic.

> *"Courage to me is doing something daring, no matter how afraid, insecure, intimidated, alone, unworthy, incapable, ridiculed, or whatever other paralyzing emotion you might feel. Courage is taking action … no matter what. So you're afraid? Be afraid. Be scared silly to the point you're trembling and nauseous, but do it anyway!"*
>
> *—Richelle E. Goodrich[3]*

Brave Challenge #1: Engage

Now I'm going to ask you to engage your brave. Using the three elements I described above—resilience, truth-telling, and action—I'm asking you to:

◊ Commit to reading this entire book. Don't place it on the shelf and forget about it. Instead, have resilience to finish what you've begun.

◊ Look within yourself and ask, "Where am I failing to act with courage? Where do I need to be braver?" Tell yourself the truth as you know it to be.

◊ Take one action step which moves you forward toward your goals and dreams. Buy a journal or write in the one you have, hire a coach, join the gym, or de-clutter your home. Whatever you've been avoiding, take a brave step of action today.

> *Courage is being scared to death, but saddling up anyway.*
>
> *—John Wayne*

Chapter Three

Where Brave Hearts Hide
The Covering of Our True Self

We each have an invisible bag on us. We spend the first few years of life putting everything in there that our friends and family don't like about us and the rest of our lives trying to retrieve it.

—Poet Robert Bly

If you've ever contemplated the question, "Who am I? I mean, honestly, who am I really?" then you're tracking with almost every woman who reaches midlife. This mid-season raises feelings of uncertainty and confusion. If you find the courage to explore that question and discover the answers, you're unlike most others. You're uncommon, even exceptional. Well done, Brave Heart.

Unfortunately, fear keeps most women stuck and unfulfilled, afraid to explore the depths of who *else* they are. They never tap their full *next* potential. Although they say they want more out of life, the idea of surrendering to growth and transformation scares them. Change might mean discomfort as they travel past the cushy familiar to peek into the scary unknown.

Don't let scary stuff stop you. Grab your brave and stay with me. Because in this chapter, I invite you to an expedition—a contemplative look inside that *invisible bag* to discover if the true essence of who you are has been captured, incarcerated, and stuffed out of view.

Joseph Campbell says, "The cave you're afraid to enter holds the treasure that you seek." Whether it's a cave, a bag, or any other secret dark place, the treasures of your life are found in the places you've been afraid to face. It's time to reclaim all of who you are so you can thrive. I don't want you to enter the most significant time of your life, unable to flourish because you're wrapped tight in fear and insecurity.

Childhood Lessons

You might have guessed we'd start this trip in childhood.

There, invisible yet monumental impressions happen *to us* and *in us*. We layer up.

What does layer up mean? Well, as experiences in life unfold, our brain searches for "meanings" surrounding each memorable event.

We ask, "Why did this happen? What did I do wrong? Why me? How can I never feel this way again?"

The mind craves answers. So, we craft stories—consciously and unconsciously—to help us make sense of and survive our world. The stories or answers we concoct become narratives, which powerfully program our brain. We draw conclusions about ourselves and our lives— what is safe or unsafe and whether we're free to evolve and grow or if we must live small and blend into the background. We decide if we deserve good or are unworthy and disqualified. We accept judgments, shame-filled thoughts, and "rules" for how we should or shouldn't operate.

I had the privilege of hearing a message from Dr. Caroline Leaf, a communication pathologist and cognitive neuroscientist. In her talk, she said, "Every experience we have goes into the brain, body, and mind and is encoded in all three domains. Our thoughts look like trees in the mind. Thoughts have root memories and branch memories. Root memories are what's (really) happening, and the branch memories are the interpretation. We have a huge forest (of memories) in our brains."

Along the way, we've also undoubtedly experienced some pain and heartache, trauma and suffering, adversity, grief and sorrow, further disrupting our development. All these encounters add up to the script we've written for ourselves.

That's where the implications get convoluted. These self-composed scripts threaten our well-being because the *messages* or *beliefs* we take from life's painful events almost always decimate our self-worth. Our childish mind does not know how to interpret happenings from truth and wisdom. How could we? Instead, we kids look inward and conclude, *I'm wrong. It's my fault. I'll do better.* And suppose no loving parent or caretaker is attuned to our pain and available to comfort us. In that case, we internalize all the lies, faulty logic, made-up stories, and harmful conclusions as incriminating evidence.

I'll share an example of this from my life.

When I was an adolescent (I don't have total recall of my age), I experienced trauma and violation. Each abusive event was confusing and horrible. Those moments changed me emotionally and biologically. Years after the events ended, and I was safe and secure, emotional scars remained. I reinforced and relived my trauma because of the story I had unconsciously concocted. *You should be ashamed of yourself. You let this happen, and now you'll never measure up. You're unworthy of love and undeserving of a successful life.* Although I never spoke those words over myself, I believed them. I took on the identity of a broken and permanently flawed girl. Instead of realizing something bad *happened to me*, I constructed the event to mean *I am something bad.* That distinction impacted everything about my self-esteem.

Famous professor, lecturer, and author, Brene' Brown is known for her research on shame and vulnerability. In her book *Rising Strong*, she makes this statement.

> *In the absence of data, we will always make up stories. It's how we are wired. In fact, the need to make up a story, especially when we are hurt, is part of our most primitive survival wiring. Meaning-making is in our biology, and our default is often to come up with a story that makes sense, feels familiar, and offers us insight into how best to self-protect.* [4]

Meanings mean everything.

If you enjoyed a carefree, magical, and wonderful childhood, you're blessed. But even in the best circumstances, we don't always get it right. Insecurity, jealousy, fear, and the innate need to perform still cause us to create *meanings* out of life's events. These *meanings* rarely align with God's truth. If you had a childhood fraught with frightful realities, you undoubtedly can pinpoint some negative core beliefs engrained in your soul. Childhood taught you facts about life you wish you had never seen or learned.

Either way, whether yours was a nurturing and beautiful childhood or a painful and brutal beginning, psychologists tell us that around the age of seven, we've established an *understanding* of how the world works, what an ideal and perfect person looks like, and how we believe we measure up. And measuring up is a matter of life and death, or so we believe. It's how we survive. So, we accept without question the lies, labels, and limits about ourselves to cope.

That's how hiding begins.

We camouflage the parts of our authentic self that don't seem to fit, or please, or matter, and hide her under layers of protective coverings. Thus, the false self is born.

In the influential book *Emotionally Healthy Spirituality*, by Pastor Peter Scazzero, he says,

> *At times our false self has become such a part of who we are that we don't even realize it. The consequences—fear, self-protection, possessiveness, manipulation, self-destructive tendencies, self-promotion, self-indulgence, and a need to distinguish ourselves from others—are harder to hide.* [5]

Is it possible you've traded in your authentic self?

Am I Enough?

Once we've consciously and unconsciously invented meanings, our beliefs, and conclusions about our life and personhood, we've also decided on the two universal questions that drive us as humans: Am I enough? Am I loved?

Since God designed you and me as relational creatures, we desperately long for love and belonging. It's in our created DNA. Those intense cravings often manifest as the two greatest fears we humans encounter, "What if I am not enough?" and "What if I am not worthy of love?"

Celebrated life coach Tony Robbins says,

> *All human beings have fears. Be it the President of United States, top athletes, actors, actresses, billionaires; everybody, at some point in time, faces the fear that they are not enough in some context. Not smart enough, not*

*pretty enough, not strong enough, not rich enough, not
funny enough... and you may not be feeling that right
now in your life, but we all feel that. And it brings up a
deeper fear, that if I am not enough, I will not be loved.
And love is like the oxygen for the soul. If somebody
does not that have that sense of aliveness and love inside
them, they feel dead inside.*[6]

We fear the loss of love and belonging. It drives us to conform. To find that invisible bag, and start shedding and stuffing our unique characteristics, which others may not understand.

And we've been doing it—conforming—since infancy.

A smile on a caretaker's face produces a smile on the baby. Watch an infant mirror daddy's facial expression or conveyed emotion. She lights up with joy and giggles with delight after receiving dad's loving affirmation. We don't realize it, of course, but the smiles, hugs, kisses, and squeezes we received as infants actively hard-wired our brains. We learned, "Do more of this and receive the love."

Conversely, when our mother's face scowled, her voice on edge and terse, we tensed and cowered and cried with rejection. We programmed that information into our brains. "Oh, no love here. Do no more of this."

We learned to perform whatever behavior won us the love and acceptance we craved.

As older children, we noticed the shaming reaction of parents, adults, siblings, and friends when we did something that didn't measure up. Parents blushed and quickly corrected us, while siblings snorted, chuckled, and made fun. Friends whispered and gossiped, removing themselves from our affiliation. And what did we learn? We learned how painful it is to be ostracized, and we felt the sting of shame, embarrassment, and the loss of love and acceptance.

We emerged from childhood as adolescents with the need and skills to fit in and belong. When we feared we would not be accepted, we successfully layered up our personalities, behaviors, and opinions—

anything rare and distinctive that made us an original—with coverings to hide our true essence. If the price of being delightfully quirky or even brilliant meant we'd lose acceptance and possibly love, then that price was just too high to pay.

Tragically, we pack up everything that makes us a one-of-a-kind masterpiece and hide it from the world. We despise what's extraordinary about us and wish it weren't so.

We mask and hide and offer the world a more acceptable version of us. A version we feel will bring better results, more love, and security. Yet in packing up, we also surrender our passions and gifts, exchanging our genius for generic.

> *The one thing that you have that nobody else has is you. Your voice, your mind, your story, your vision. So, write and draw and build and play and dance and live as only you can.*
>
> —Neil Gaiman

To boost your confidence, visit

https://www.braveheartedwoman.com/ignite_your_confidence_ebook

People Pleasing

Has the fear of losing love and belonging created pressure for you to live a life that's not authentically yours?

If you were reared in shame and judgment, you no doubt have become (or were at one time) tethered to people-pleasing instead of living from your heart. And to add to that addiction to please others, many religious messages contributed to our belief that we should, as good

Christian women, put other's wants first, say yes to all worthy causes, and lay our interests down to serve those in need. It's all great stuff, but at what cost? Sometimes, we pay the price of fulfilling our God-given assignments with our whole, authentic, redeemed self.

For years, I set aside my calling to please others. The fear of man was pretty grand in my life, and I often let what I thought others expected of me to rule my life. "Women aren't allowed to be pastors, preachers, or leaders of men," people told me more than once. Although my heart burned like fire shut up in my bones, I tried to snuff it out and hide the embers. Shame coiled around my mind whispering, *who do you think you are? God doesn't use women.* Hiding the light seemed like the only answer.

> *Your need for acceptance keeps you invisible in this world.*
> —Comedian Jim Carey

While traveling to a conference, I recently viewed a documentary about singing sensation Whitney Houston, who had the most incredible God-touched voice of the century. In one poignant scene, saxophonist Kirk Whalum gave a gripping interview. He had toured with Whitney for more than seven years and befriended the singer.

Here's a quote from Kirk Whalum in that scene.

> *Whitney's favorite saying was, can I be me? That was the conundrum: [She would say] "I've made all this money and all these people happy, and I still can't be me." When you create somebody or something, at some point that something realizes, this isn't me. I've been created and molded into this, and they break out of it.* [7]

Later in the same documentary, Whitney said, "You gotta know who you are before you step into this business because if you're trying to find it, you'll probably wind up being somebody else, somebody you probably don't even like."[8]

Whitney felt the pressure to conform and hide her authentic self, trapped in a persona that wasn't her own. In the end, that pressure took her life.

Fear, Shame, and Hiding

Hiding is not new. Ever since shame slithered into the Garden of Eden, fear of fully being known has coiled around the heart of every human born. From the first bite of the apple, the vulnerable couple's eyes opened, and they scurried to find fig leaves. To do what? To cover their unique differences. Fear, shame, and hiding became the sentence of us all, the sentence of you.

So, let's talk about you.

In what ways have you played small, shrinking to avoid disapproval? What parts of you are stuffed inside that *invisible bag* that, if you had the courage, you'd retrieve? Have you lost yourself, your personality, and your genuine self in an attempt to conform to the expectations of others? Or perhaps you've placed expectations on yourself. You've compared yourself to others, fearful you won't measure up. You want to please people and find acceptance, because that's how you experience love and value.

Reflect again on our two greatest fears: We fear we are inadequate and that people won't love us. Has your brave-heart been swallowed up in fear? You may be donning a false self.

The False Self

"How do I know if I'm clad in a false self?" you ask.

Well, like protective bandages covering a wound, the false self wraps the authentic, redeemed self. See if you can detect the characteristics of the false self. Do any of these describe you?

The False Self:

◊   is detached from deep self-awareness.

◊   feels unclear and blurry about a vision for life.

◊   is wrapped in duplicity, misaligned between what I say I value and how I behave.

◊   determines life goals from sources without. What do others expect of me? What will give me the most accolades?

◊   easily conforms to the pressure of others.

◊   needs affirmations to boost self-esteem.

◊   avoids criticism and views feedback as rejection.

◊   looks to others for value and vicariously draws purpose from them.

In contrast, the authentic version wears a God-confidence. We drop the fig leaves to find God has beautifully covered us.

The Authentic Self:

◊   is attached to keen self-awareness.

◊   identifies a clear vision for life.

◊   detects misalignment between what I say I value and how I behave.

◊   determines life goals from within, and trusts inner desires.

◊   respects others but doesn't easily conform to their expectations.

◊   enjoys affirmation, but the need for affirmations doesn't drive decisions.

◊   doesn't crumble under criticism and rejection.

◊   dares to live God's purpose.

Letting Go of Fear

It's a scary notion to let go of the false self. *What if I feel naked? What if, for the first time, I feel alive?* It's time to banish fear.

Fear takes a large life and makes it small. When fear, insecurity, timidity, worry, anxiety, dread, and all of fear's many cousins plague our life, we lose our freedom, our aliveness, and sense of adventure. We consent to a life lived with self-imposed limits and stifling boundaries. If you've experienced trauma, you especially want the safety of certainty, stability, and routine. Predictability helps you regulate your emotions. Even though your day-to-day existence may be mundane, perhaps even unhealthy, you feel assured of your ability to navigate. Life is unsurprisingly routine.

But it's also small.

Here's where I decree a *no* over you. God has more for you than small, my sister.

God wants to free you from the fear that keeps you chained to a false self with an average existence. In the making of a bravehearted woman, your next step is to claim the life God has for you. Unleash your brave, stand toe to toe with fear, and say, "I'm going to go for it. I'm afraid, but feelings of fear must move aside and get out of my way because I will take this step, make this decision, take the plunge, begin the change, and dive into the waters of an extraordinary life."

Tony Robbins' famous quote says: "Change happens when the pain of staying the same is greater than the pain of change."

If this chapter describes you and the pain of staying the same has reached a pinnacle, I'm excited to tell you change is possible. Genuine transformation is on the way, should you choose it. You can prosper and succeed in midlife.

First, however, let me prepare you. On the road to growth and development, you'll likely encounter two paths to transformation. One path will lead you to the change you long for and the other path will send you back around the mountain for another lap. These "emotional change cycles" describe what happens in your psychology during change. Understanding the cycles beforehand will equip you with stamina as you navigate new terrain.

Coaches Joel and Natalie Rivera, Founders of Transformation Academy, (https://transformationacademy.com/, n.d.) describe the scenario of the first path. In their "cycle of change," they've researched and documented what happens to us emotionally within the change process.

Phase one is **Discontent**. Here, we grow increasingly unhappy and discontent with life. We tolerate and ignore the circumstance or issue because it's all we know—familiar, and familiar is comfortable. We hang in there because we fear changes.

The next phase is the **Breaking Point**. This phase happens when our level of discontent builds high enough to bring emotional pain. We are exhausted, disgusted, or triggered by a dramatic event that brings us to the breaking point.

Decision is the third phase of the change cycle. We're ready to change and declare we will no longer tolerate the undesirable situation. We take the first step toward change, giving us a short-lived sense of hope and a healthy dopamine shot.

The fourth phase is **Fear**. Rather quickly, if not immediately, feelings of empowerment subside, and we encounter fear. Fear seizes us, and we feel uncomfortable and anxious about changing. We doubt our decision. Options look bleak. *Do I keep going or return to what I know?* We feel helpless and empty.

Phase five is called **Amnesia**. The fear of change grows strong enough to make the beginning situation appear better than initially understood. We perceive our former circumstances as less anxiety-producing than the change. I's comfortable. It's familiar. Old issues have become part of our identity, so we resist transformation and temporarily forget why we wanted to change.

Finally, in Phase 6, **<u>Backtracking</u>** takes place. Most women choose to go back or stick with the issue they longed to change. They rationalize and talk themselves out of change.

In this scenario, we don't fully apprehend change because fear and backtracking interrupt the forward progress. Humans like to return to what is comfortable, even when "comfortable" is dysfunctional and miserable.

Notice what happened to Laura when she entered the cycle of change:

Laura could bear it no longer. (Discontent) At almost 300 pounds, her knees, feet, heart, and back were in constant pain. *This weight has to come off, or I'm going to die.* (Breaking Point) Laura had reached her *enough* moment and decided to change her circumstance. *I am not going to live like this anymore,* she determined. (Decision)

Arming herself with an exercise and eating plan, Laura took the first brave step down the path to transformation. Her enthusiasm and hope carried her for the first few weeks, reminding herself often, *I didn't put this weight on overnight, and it won't come off overnight. I will be patient with myself.* But as time passed, determination waned, and self-discipline crumbled. (Fear) Soon, fear of failure and the voice of rationalization crept in; *What if this doesn't work for me? What if my body just can't let go of the fat? I am probably insulin resistant. I've been big-boned since I was little. I'm going to be overweight for the rest of my life. If people can't love me for who I am, they're not real friends. Fat women are sexy.* (Amnesia)

Laura convinced herself her condition was just her "lot in life." Once she entertained those lying negative beliefs, it wasn't long before she gave up her weight loss incentive and hopelessly returned to her old habits. (Backtracking)

Can you see what happened to Laura? She fell prey to the difficult phase in the cycle of change.

With God's help, however, we can have a new ending to our old problems. Another path or change cycle occurs for the dedicated, informed, and accountable woman who desires life-changing transformation.

I've created the following Cycle of Change for my clients:

Phase 1- Behold the Vision

Discontent. Growing exceedingly dissatisfied with something in your life. You've reached your "enough" moment and want your pain to stop. That's a great start—you can articulate what you *don't* want anymore. For real and lasting change, however, you must do more than decide what you don›t want. You must discover what you want and where you'd rather be. To create a life you love, you must have a vision. What do you desire for your future? Get a beautiful picture in your mind of where you'd rather be. As the true adage goes, "You'll never leave where you are until you decide where you'd rather be."

Phase 2- Beginning Backbone

"Starting" should be rewarded. It can be challenging.

Here you make a firm decision and commitment to start something new—something you desperately want. Your fresh start is exhilarating, and you're energized. Although scary, you determine to change, even while afraid. You've traded your *wishbone* for *backbone*. Now, with a renewed imagination, ideas swirl and fill the vision board of your heart. You're firmly dedicated and convinced that you'll win this time. Motivation is at an all-time high, and you're employing new habits and actions. However, this optimism is temporary. If you're not prepared, the third phase of change can drain your positive resolve.

Phase 3- Beliefs and Barriers

In phase two, you've started new habits. Habits, when first implemented, are similar to the hairs on your midlife head—thin, delicate, and fragile.

Over time these "hairs" or neuro pathways in your brain, increase and grow thick, like a ponytail or strong cable. Soon after you start your new beginning, your brain detects (or detests) something is different. You've left your comfort zone and stepped into the unfamiliar. According to your brain, whose job is to identify threats and keep you safe and secure, you've entered the *danger zone*. Before you destroy an old but cable-sized neuro pathway and create a new one, your brain wants to drag you back to the safety of sameness.

So, in phase three, you'll encounter limiting beliefs and rationalizations rising to bully your mind back to former programming. Excuses will push to the forefront of thought, persuading you to hold on to the patterns and routines your brain has always known.

Relentlessly.

But remember how we build muscles? We build them by using resistance. When you feel challenging barriers of resistance, celebrate. You're on the verge of a beautiful transformation. Instead of listening to the deceptive rationalization of your logical lizard brain, push back, press on, and trust that change is taking place. Let your brain know that your *thinking mind* is the authority.

Phase 4- Become or Boomerang

In this phase, fundamental transformation occurs. You're shedding your old identity.

You're sensing changes, and you like the results. The pain of your former issue is significantly reduced or gone, and you're reaping positive benefits from your decision to change. You have fresh hope, empowered by your new-found reality. You see what you want from life, not just what you don't want. You've created a vibrant life, a life you're proud of. You've earned the reward, and you love it.

Fundamental transformation doesn't mean limiting beliefs and barriers no longer batter your mind. It means the joy and value of transformation overpower fears and excuses to remain stuck. You will arrive at your desired destination if you don't sabotage your efforts.

Phase 5- Brave New Identity

If you reach phase five, you've successfully installed new habits and beliefs. You possess a vision for yourself and a capable, confident identity that knows anything is possible. You've become new.

Human beings are not born once and for all on the day their mothers give birth to them, but ... life obliges them over and over again to give birth to themselves.

—Gabriel García Márquez

If you long for this kind of transformation in your life, if you're ready to shed the layers of the false self and step into midlife with the new authentic self, clothed in the outfit the Lord has prepared for you, then agree with me in this prayer and get ready for your wardrobe change.

Brave Challenge #2: Shed

Pray this prayer for the next 7 days.

Father God, today, I agree to relinquish the layers of protection and pride that clothe the false self. I choose, instead, the brave awakening of my authentic core to fully live true to who you have created me to be. Reveal to me the ways I hide and pretend. I remind myself that I am safe and secure in you. I step out of the shadowy self- into the light of the true-self, clothed with your glory. Amen

NOW I STEP

Today I am a soul set free.

I dream, I choose, I believe in my future.

I am brave. I am determined. I am powerful.

NOW,

I step into the New Me.

I am no victim. I am not lost. I am not defeated.

I am a daughter of purpose; God's called, chosen, and beloved.

NOW

I see with eyes of vision.

I clearly walk the path God has for me.

NOW

My mind is made up. I am determined. There's no looking back.

With fierce execution I step into God's plan.

I seize the moment.

Now.

I Become.

—Dawn Scott Damon

Where Brave Hearts Rise: The Awakening

What makes the muskrat guard his musk? Courage. What makes the Sphinx the 7th Wonder? Courage. What makes the dawn come up like thunder? Courage.

—Cowardly Lion

What would you do if your soul was free from the drag of fear; if curiosity and courage replaced scary stories and whispers of doom?

You would rise.

If you conquered fear and silenced lying voices, you would catch the wind and rise to new challenges. You'd be curious enough to explore the adventurous beginnings of an authentic life and brave enough to accept living unwrapped. When faced with intimidation and criticism, you would put your head up, face the stars, and rise.

Once curiosity awakens you to what is possible, you'd enter the revolution that transformation inevitably ignites and you would rise with fortitude, making complicated, messy, but oh-so-beautiful changes.

That's what bravehearted women do.

It's Your Time to Rise

By definition, "Rise" is a verb that means moving from a lower position to a higher level, elevating, coming up, or going up. The word also means to awaken.

In arriving at midlife—the crisis of the crossroads—the invitation is for you to rise and shine.

With neglect to your fear, rising brave means you're willing to stay fervently engaged. You're willing to peel back the layers of the false self and come out of hiding. You've circled the same monotonous mountain long enough. You're ready to shed old attitudes, bad habits, toxic relationships and meager mindsets. Mediocrity no longer defines you. You're excited to set your true self free. Rising means you're prepared to break through barriers and ascend to new heights.

But what if rising is uncomfortable?

I hear the question, and I acknowledge your hesitancy! So, let me assure you here and now—you will definitely be uncomfortable. The opportunity to live authentically is not without risk. Rising as a bravehearted woman will require uncomfortable action accompanied by uncomfortable emotions. As I've often said, midlife is not for the faint of heart. It takes courage to honestly explore our current life and choose to re-invent.

Sometimes we'll relate more to the cowardly lion. The dawn won't always come up like thunder, but it will always come up. You can do something today to move you toward living from your heart. Take one bandage off at a time. As Eleanor Roosevelt said, *"Do one thing every day that scares you."*

Practice getting comfortable with the uncomfortable. Recognize that feeling foolishly awkward and vulnerable is a part of taking new and higher territory in your life. Brian Tracy, a motivational speaker who has written over 80 books on personal growth and development, says, "You can only grow if you are willing to feel awkward and uncomfortable with trying something new." I want you to realize, however, that uncomfortable doesn't mean unsafe; it doesn't mean you've made a bad decision or are heading in the wrong direction.

If you feel destabilized, rest assured; it's normal and temporary. Tell yourself often, "*This step of uncomfortable but courageous action is awakening my brain to accept something new. That means I'm growing and changing!*" Be excited when you encounter resistance—you're challenging your brain to move past the safety zone.

*"Take chances, make mistakes. That's how you grow.
Pain nourishes your courage. You have to fail in order to
practice being brave."*

—*Mary Tyler Moore*

So where are you being called to rise? In what areas of your life do you need to become brave and step out of your comfort zone to reclaim the life intended for you? Where has fear encroached upon you, shrinking the borders of your life and influence, exerting more power over you than you imagined?

Expose fear as the liar it is!

If you think:

◊   you're not enough

◊   you're unworthy of love

◊   you're an imposter

◊   you're never going to change

◊   there is no beautiful future for you

You can bet fear is plotting against you.

Those sinister lies drift through your mind, looking for a place to lodge. Let them remain drifters, my sister. There is no truth in news from hell.

Instead of giving fear undue power in your life, endure uncomfortable seasons, and prepare to rise.

Fear stifles our experience of being alive.

—Maggie Warrell

4 Traits of the Courageous

It takes courage to rise.

Courage. It originally comes from the Latin word *Cor,* meaning heart.

Living with courage is living with all your heart. It's living out your dreams despite the presence of doubt and fear, willing to risk failure to be true to yourself and the authentic person God created you to be.

Being terrified but going ahead and doing what must be done—that's courage. The one who feels no fear is a fool, and the one who lets fear rule him is a coward.

—Author, Piers Anthony

In the Bible, there's a story about a man named Joshua. God told him to be courageous. The command wasn't a pep talk to bolster confidence. No, God was calling Joshua to shift his thinking from defeat to victory, to change the narrative in his mind from cowardice to bravery. In other words, God told Joshua, "*Choose* courage!" (See Joshua 1:6-9).

That's right. Courage is not just an emotion that comes to a select few. We can all choose courage despite the emotions of fear and timidity.

The key is in the *shift*.

Humans have the habit of focusing on the negative side of any challenge or opportunity. According to neuroscience, our brain is twice as sensitive to loss than potential gain. Our brain is hardwired to stay safe, so our negative internal dialogue starts to rationalize saying something like this; *This isn't going to work. What if I fail? It's too complicated; I can't do it.* We focus on what will go wrong and what we stand to lose. With defeatist chatter in our heads, no wonder we remain paralyzed, with no inertia to live out our dreams. In truth, we're not staying safe, we're staying stuck.

Ah, but when we shift, we change our perspective from what we stand to lose to what we stand to gain. The shift in perspective helps us to fix our attention on the outcome, the reward. Courage rises within us, and bravery grows due to right thinking. Our 'courage choice' becomes easier when we tell ourselves a better story.

God calls you to pursue your bold, brave vision. Don't lose out on life's opportunities and open doors because of a brave heart deficit. Like Joshua, you must be *very strong* and courageous to capture God›s purpose for your life. Conquering fear is critical to your assignment.

Here are four actions you'll need to take to muster your courage:

1. Name Your Fear

Admit and acknowledge your fear and give it a name. Then, ask yourself, "What specifically am I afraid of?"

Be precise in defining the fear you struggle with. When you evaluate and name your fear, you contain it. You'll discover that the thing you dread has limits.

—Mark Twain

2. Act, Even When You're Afraid

As I've written already, the *emotion* of fear won't leave you altogether. Fear comes to us all, flying over our heads like a bird in flight. But you still have the power of choice when fear does swarm over you—let it build a nest in your head and peck away at your brain, or capture and cage it. Sometimes, feelings of fear serve a good purpose. So don't ignore your emotions. But don't wait to take action steps until you have NO fear. March on BraveHeart!

*Go back?" he thought. "No good at all! Go sideways?
Impossible! Go forward? Only thing to do! On we go!" So
up he got and trotted along with his little sword held in
front of him and one hand feeling the wall, and his heart
all of a patter and a pitter.*

—J.R.R. Tolkien

3. Focus on the Win

*Man cannot discover new oceans unless he has the courage
to lose sight of the shore.*

—Lord Chesterfield

In every pursuit of honorable goals, you must define the win. What do you want to accomplish? Be clear on what you hope to gain, and then keep your heart focused on the benefits. Jesus endured the temporary pain and suffering of the cross because of the joy awaiting him. He knew a permanent and victorious outcome was worth the sacrifice. See Hebrews 12:2

You, too, have victory ahead of you if you endure. Keep your eyes on the prize and ask yourself:

- ◊ How will the quality of my life improve when I gain victory?

- ◊ What accomplishments will I make, and how will they impact my world?

- ◊ How will I be able to serve others?

4. Show Up

Sometimes all you can do is show up. I've seen bravery melt like wax when we overthink a problem. Too much analysis elevates anxiety and causes procrastination. Instead, don't underestimate the incredible value of taking one small step at a time. Just show up, and the rest will unfold.

Inch by inch, everything's a cinch. Yard by yard it can really be hard.

—The Worm

Courage determines the perimeters of your life. You'll expand boundaries and increase in every area of your life through brave and bold living.

Haven't I commanded you? Strength! Courage! Don't be timid; don't get discouraged. God, your God, is with you every step you take.

—Joshua 1:9 THE MESSAGE

Comfortable with the Uncomfortable

Now that I've encouraged you, I must also prepare you!

When you choose to become brave and rise, moving out of what may be a rut, you'll undergo another kind of turbulence. It's the commotion change creates. Not everyone will celebrate your decision to elevate. When you shed the layers of your false self, others connected to you feel off-balanced as they watch your old protective coatings fall to the side. You were once predictable and safely unmotivated, but now you have unfettered your limits and turned the "rules" upside down. Don't be surprised when loved ones squawk more than support.

What are you doing? Tossing doubt your way.

We like the old you better. We don't accept the new you. Rejection.

Who do you think you are? You should be ashamed. Manipulation.

Your change has, by necessity, brought undesired change to those around you, and some don't like it. Becoming brave, however, demands that you let go of worrying about what others think of you and release yourself from meeting everyone's expectations.

Again, this from Maggie Warrell:

> *On occasion, we have to buck others' expectations, defy what they think what we 'should' do and risk their disapproval, disappointment or even rejection.*

She says,

> *Far too often we give other people's fears, preferences, and desires undue sway in our lives. It doesn't serve us or them.*

I don't want to imply that we disregard the concern or wise counsel of others in our lives. Not at all. But by now, most midlife women have done the lion's share of caring for everyone else. Perhaps you're caring for grandchildren, children, or elderly parents even as you read this. I understand and believe that God invites us into seasons of selfless serving. Often, however, women who have set themselves on the back burner of their life without taking the time to cultivate their personal growth and development find themselves empty, even resentful when their caretaking season is over. Too many women look in the mirror and say, *"I don't know you."* They admit they're lost and unsure about their life. They regret neglecting their God-given purpose. So, yes, sometimes you have to push back on the expectations of others and resist any guilt that tries to woo you back to the status quo.

The deep interior and exterior work of transformation both call us to become brave.

When we chose to begin to make changes in our life, the pressure can feel like either our inner person, or exterior life relationships will implode in the process. That shaking that happens in our life, can be compared, I believe for each of us, to breaking the sound barrier for the first time. Both require great courage.

The above quote from Peter Scazzero continues about how taking the journey into living out of our true selves will require us pressing through that shaking and remaining faithful, much like when Chuck Yeager finally broke the sound barrier.

On October 14th, 1947, U.S. Air Force Captain Chuck Yeager became the first person to fly faster than the speed of sound. For many years before that, aviators believed it was impossible to fly faster than the speed of sound. They stuck to the notion that the "transonic drag rise" or velocity would rip the aircraft apart.

The conclusion?

They determined man would never fly faster than the speed of sound, nor was he meant to. Until that is, Chuck Yeager climbed aboard the "Glamorous Glennis," the aircraft named after his wife, sunk into the crowded cockpit, and barreled through the turbulence. What happened next changed the course of history forever. Chuck Yeager broke the sound barrier.

That story inspires me, and I've often used this illustration in my preaching. In an attempt to break the *barrier*, the violent rattling, shaking, shrieking, and vicious vibration created such volatility that in every previous attempt, pilots backed off the throttle and gave up, fearing for their lives.

Fear drains the courage out of us. When we're ready to rise to a new level, the shake, rattle, and roll within us and around us can frighten us into backing off and scurrying to our place of comfort and safety. So, we give up and conclude we're not meant to break the barriers that loom in front of us. If, however, we press through the clamor and the anxiety-producing, heart-pounding, shaking, we can break through and take new frontiers just as Chuck Yeager did.

Later, Chuck Yeager himself wrote, "I was thunderstruck. After all the anxiety, breaking the sound barrier turned out to be a perfectly paved speedway. After all the anticipation it was really a letdown. The 'unknown' was a poke through Jell-O."

Wow.

I'm not minimizing what you must face, but after years of helping women genuinely come alive, most say, "What was I so afraid of? I wish I had the guts to make this change years ago."

What we fear is the unknown and losing certainty and control. Yet fear keeps us grounded, unable to rise.

Where is the barrier in your life? Is God calling you to face the unknown and breakthrough? To poke through the Jell-O façade in front of you?

Sure, your rise will create disruption. But you've got this. All it takes is a brave heart and a little poke.

You may shoot me with your words; you may cut me with your eyes, You may kill me with your hatefulness, but still, like air, I'll rise!

—Maya Angelou

What is Your Vision?

When you consent to fear, you let it keep you from honoring your highest values and bravest vision. If you even allow yourself to connect to your bold vision. Maybe fear has stopped you from dreaming altogether. Many women still wonder, *What do I want to be when I grow up?*

Do you have a vision? We will take a deeper dive into your vision in Chapter 6.

But one way I help you discover vision for your life is through a thought-provoking exercise I call the "Older You."

Take a moment and think of your older self. You're seasoned with wisdom and have a message to share with your younger self. Can you see her? What step of brave action would she tell you to take? Where would she say, *go for it, girl, dive in, step up, double down, maximize?* What advice or encouragement would she offer to keep you from experiencing regret? Your older, wiser self wants you to live all out with abundance, victory, and success.

This exercise helps you answer the question, *what will I regret if I never take the risk and seize the moment?* We regret far more the opportunities we never took than the ones we did. So where do you need to take a leap of faith?

In the best-selling memoir, *The Top 5 Regrets of the Dying*, Bronnie Ware wrote about her transforming experience serving the dying with palliative care. She explains that common themes surfaced when questioned about any regrets her patients had or anything they would do differently. The number one regret reported was, "I wish I'd had the courage to live a life true to myself, not the life others expected of me."

This verdict was the most common regret of all.

*When people realize their life is almost over and look back
clearly on it, it is easy to see how many dreams have gone
unfulfilled. Most people had not honoured even a half of
their dreams and had to die knowing that it was due to
choices they had made, or not made.* [9]

If you have any fear, then fear regret more than you fear failure, letting someone down, or coloring outside the lines. When God fills your heart with vision, he expects you to give him your best yes.

Rachel Hollis beautifully explains every dream begins with some form of *what if.* "That what if? That's your potential knocking on the door of your heart begging it to find the courage to override all the fear in your head. That "what if" is there for a reason."[10]

I say, both your dreams and your regrets start with the same question, *what if?* Your dream bubbles inside you, floats to your heart and whispers, *What if I could … ?* Your regret, sinks to your heart's floor and yearns with endless echoes, *What if I would have … ?*

Only you can decide if your dream takes flight and soars, bringing you joy and fulfillment or if it crashes to the floor, lying dormant forever more.

*You gain strength, courage, and confidence by every
experience in which you stop to look fear in the face. You
can say to yourself, "I lived through this horror. I can take
the next thing that comes along."*

—Eleanor Roosevelt

Midlife Inventory

You've arrived at midlife. Congratulations. You've proven you're brave. But now transition, simply because of your age, is demanded of you. Why not take advantage of this natural opportunity and inventory your life? Are you still growing, learning, stretching, and blooming? Or are you stuck, stunted, and static like a car in 5:00 P.M. gridlock? God forbid. Instead, take to heart the old axiom, "When you stop growing, you start dying." Don't drift into obscurity now, at your life's richest and most valuable time. Your best and most significant season is yet ahead of you. A fearless inventory can help you identify areas where you may be in danger of losing ground and slipping into apathy. Consider questions like the ones below to help you locate where you are.

◊ Where do you feel life is calling you to come up higher? To rise brave?

◊ Are you living fully authentic or trapped in people-pleasing efforts?

◊ Does the fear of what you don't want stop you from reaching for what you want?

◊ What areas of your life need attention? Eight specific areas impact our life balance, satisfaction, and overall well-being:

- Personal Growth and Learning

- Health and Fitness- Physical, Emotional, and Mental

- Career and Purpose

- Finances

- Family and Friends

- Partner and Romance

- Spirituality

- Fun and Recreation

Where can you rise as a bravehearted woman? What does the inventory reveal to you about you?

Well, in the next section of this book, I will lead you through what I call the "Five Fortitudes of a BraveHearted Woman."

These Five Fortitudes are the characteristics of internal bravery and self-discipline—the qualities you must cultivate and possess—to elevate any deficit in your midlife inventory and create a life you're eager to live. You will grow and increase as you learn to master the Five Fortitudes. I've even used the word B.R.A.V.E. in front of each fortitude to help you grasp the ingredients of a BraveHearted woman easily.

You're Welcome.

The "5 fortitudes" are

1. **Fortitude 1: Claim a Bold Vision.** I See.

2. **Fortitude 2: Cultivate a Real Identity.** I Believe.

3. **Fortitude 3: Choose an Able Mindset.** I Think.

4. **Fortitude 4: Craft Virtuous Talk.** I Say.

5. **Fortitude 5: Commit to Excellent Actions and Habits.** I Do.

Together, we will examine your bold vision, real identity, able mindset, virtuous speech, and excellent actions and habits.

Get ready to rise …

Brave Challenge #3: Rise

Get your journal and thoroughly answer the questions posed in the Midlife Inventory above. Date the page and save it. You'll refer to your inventory to mark your progress.

Part 2: Where Brave Hearts Thrive:

The 5 Fortitudes of a BraveHearted Woman.

Learn the Brave, Virtuous, Consistently Gritty, Disciplined Habits of a Successful Midlife Woman.

Chapter Five

The Five Fortitudes of a BraveHearted Woman

Life is now in session. Are you present?

—John Maxwell

Ever since I was 8 years old, I've wanted to help girls feel happy. I wanted them to know they were beautiful, that God loved them, and that they were special. I gravitated toward the girls who were quirky and different and, therefore, unpopular and often lonely. I wanted them to feel good about themselves, their bodies, appearance, personalities, and minds. I was undoubtedly a blooming empath, loving friends from the Island of Misfit Toys.

My quest to inspire women to live their best has continued throughout the years. I help women build their self-esteem, take actions to improve their lives, and, well … live with grit and glitter!

In my late 30s, I noticed something that made a big impression on me. The circle of my friends a were women, all about 10 to 15 years older than me. With 40 on my horizon, I noted how my trail-blazing friends were tackling midlife. I made some wonderful and not-so-wonderful discoveries.

Some friends gracefully aged.

They embraced themselves as a wise, mature woman who seemed comfortable in their identity. They slowed down their involvement in activities, were satisfied with a well-lived life, and became grandmas with passive, loving souls. They allowed their hair to grey, age lines to grace their face, and ditched the stilettos for mall-walking tennis shoes. I respected it. But for me, something was missing.

Other friends fought aging.

They hiked up their skirts, found Botox, glued on false eyelashes, and injected every inch of their face with fillers. They wouldn't tell their age. They looked plastic and found fulfillment in smoothies and jazzercise. I detected these women carried shame and were embarrassed by the aging process.

I thought, hmmm, I'm not against Botox at all. But I don't want to go down that road. There has to be more.

A few friends seemed to give up altogether.

They stopped learning, growing, and from my vantage point, caring. Instead, they lost the battle of the midlife bulge, packed on the pounds, and started wearing stretch pants with long, draping blouses. They dropped out of enrichment classes, replacing them with nights binging on Netflix. If I asked what they were reading, they said they hadn't picked up a book in a long while.

Definitely not a midlife strategy for me.

Or you.

The opportunity I offer in this book is for you to consider reinventing midlife and be intentional about your "next half, best half" of life.

I want you to live full-out as a savvy, confident, regal midlife woman who stays intentional about her personal growth and development—body, soul, and spirit.

So, in the following pages, I've included what I believe are the foundational fortitudes a woman living in our season must possess.

What is Fortitude?

The word fortitude means "strength of mind and character." But here's where I take creative license and meld together some nuances of the word to create my definition.

Fortitude is formed from bravery, virtue, and consistent grit to execute with relentless discipline, the keystone habits of a successful woman.

Wow. That was a lot, right? Well, fortitude is that great.

Let me break down the definition.

If you take;

Virtue - High moral excellence and standards.

Consistent Grit – Courage and resolve to keep going. The enduring strength of character.

Keystone Habits – Habits that produce a chain of other great habits. A keystone habit is the first domino to fall, triggering a series of other positive habits.

Relentless Discipline – Making yourself do what you need to do, when you need to do it.

Now, blend those words together, and you will find fortitude.

The Five Fortitudes

Let's start with a brief overview of the Five Fortitudes, and then we will take a deeper dive in to each one.

Fortitude 1. Claim a Bold Vision. I see.

In this first transformational step of the journey, you'll learn the life-changing power of vision and how it guides you and acts like a magnet to bring you to your destiny. Without a vision, people perish. In this fortitude, you will awaken your distinctive vision and claim your purpose.

Fortitude 2. Cultivate a Real Identity. I believe.

A confident identity is a powerful identity. What you believe about yourself—your identity—will create the outcomes you receive. In Fortitude 2, you'll learn how to build a confident identity so you can reach your dreams. Step out of insecurity, fear, indecision, and low self-worth and into an identity that empowers you, makes you brave, and gives you energy for a successful life.

Fortitude 3. Choose an Able Mindset. I think.

Your unconscious mind commands 80% of the direction of your life. That's because we are often unaware of our thoughts and habitual actions. Refuse toxic thinking, false beliefs, and negative outlooks to govern you.

Instead, renew your mindset. If you change your thoughts, you'll change your life. Fortitude 3 gives you the Seven Mindsets you need.

Fortitude 4. Craft Virtuous Talk. I say.

There is so much more to our words than what we have understood. Neuroscience now confirms what God has declared. Our words create our worlds. Do you know how to speak affirmations to bless you and bring into your life the good you desire vs. the negative words you say, which curse and steal your success?

Fortitude 5. Commit to Excellent Actions. I Do.

If you don't have a strategic plan and take *action*, you will stay stuck. There is a skill to effective goal-setting and goal-getting. *Habits* will help you move forward. Learn the science and watch it work for you.

These are the brave, virtuous, and gritty fortitudes of a successful woman. Oh, I forgot to add … and we do them all with glitter!

Brave Challenge #4: Commit

You're about to dive into transformation. On a scale from 1-10, how ready are you to make this *your* journey and not just a book you're reading?

What can you do to commit to being all-in?

Chapter Six

Fortitude 1: Claim a Bold Vision.
I See

The path from dreams to success does exist. May you have the vision to find it, the courage to get on to it, and the perseverance to follow it.

—Kalpana Chawla 1st Indian Astronau*t*

*E*verything begins with a vision.

As I write this chapter, excitement floods me. I feel passion, like fire blazing within me. Why, you ask? Because I'm convinced the power of this Fortitude—awakening and claiming your vision—is transformative, I'm already celebrating the positive changes you're about to experience. I'm that confident you're going to grow. So, instead of saying, "Buckle-up and get secure for the ride," I will cheer you on by saying, "Let go, unleash, and prepare to soar, my BraveHearted Sister." Vision is about to explode in you and unlock the shackles, which have tried to keep you grounded. It's your time to fly.

Awaken to Your Vision

First, understand and believe God created vision. It's his idea. When he made a promise to Abraham, God took Abe outside to show him the stars in the sky and the sand on the shore. Then he told him, "I promise that I will give you as many descendants as there are stars in the sky or grains of sand along the seashore." (My paraphrase. See Genesis 22:17). What was God doing? He gave Abraham a vision, a picture of his future.

In the same way, God wants to give you a picture, a vision of what is coming. Vision is how your Creator invites you into His promise for your life. So, when you allow yourself to imagine big and behold a picture, you're claiming and positioning yourself to experience the dream God has ordained for you.

Where there is no vision, people perish.

—Proverbs 29:18

Vision awakens you and bids you *come alive.* Once awakened to what is possible for your life, you've lit a stick of dynamite in your soul. The inspiration vision creates becomes explosive. Vision is the fuel that drives us, the fire that motivates us to pursue our dreams and goals. Only with vision aflame will we live full out, blazing with joy and zeal. So, consider the following words as me helping you blow on that ember inside you; *Rise and shine. Now is the time to awaken to your dream and purpose. You are worthy of living a grand, beautiful, brave life, and it (re-) ignites here and now. Today is your moment to uncover, create, cultivate, and claim your vision!*

Everything begins with a vision.

Now that vision has inspired us, let's define it more fully. Vision is an inner picture, dream, and representation of the desired "Future You," accompanied by a driving, compelling, burning desire to achieve what you see. Another definition of mine for vision is "The hopes and dreams that bubble up when you awaken your mind and allow your imagination to come alive and see what is possible." As Albert Einstein said, "Imagination is everything. It is the preview of life's coming attraction."

Your vision is a picture of life's coming attractions for *you*. Your vision is unlike everyone else's dream. Your vision is unique to you. It's how you answer the "why and what" of your life; *Why am I here? What gives me meaning?* Don't expect everyone to understand what you see. Just keep dreaming. Suppose you have a relentless aspiration that won't die, a never-ending knocking on your heart's door, the seeds of something planted in you that won't be refused. In that case, the dormant vision wants to come alive.

When I was young, my two older sisters and I played church. Our maternal and paternal grandfathers were pastors, so our parents ensured we were always in church twice on Sunday. We loved imitating what we saw by creating our version of a Sunday morning service. We delegated my middle sister Debbie as the song leader. She has incredible musical talent. And for head usher, we doled that job out to my oldest sister Denise. She still is our boss. I was the orator. I loved speaking, preaching, and standing before my congregation of two.

Little did I know God was sparking my life's purpose through our childhood fun. It never occurred to me that I would become a pastor one day. I never saw women in ministry or behind the pulpit. Yet, I had images of myself standing before the church's people, bringing a message.

At age 28, my dream of preaching was still there, burning inside me. One day, with great trepidation, I shared my vision with a close girlfriend, "I believe God is calling me to become a pastor and to preach." I can still see the shock and disbelief on her face as she fell to the floor, rolling in laughter. To her, my dream was outlandish, ridiculous, impossible. She couldn't comprehend how an audacious vision like mine could ever come to pass.

That day was a crash course with two lessons. First, keep your dreams private from those who have no spiritual imagination or prophetic vision. It's futile to convince average minds of greatness. Second, if I was going to see the fruition of my vision, I would have to fight to keep my dream alive. God gave this picture to me—no one else. I was the steward of the promise. I would feed the vision, fan the flame, and continue to take courageous action steps. More on this topic in chapters to come. But can you imagine my joy the day I was ordained and licensed to preach? It was indeed an audacious dream come true.

The Power of Vision

Vision is power-packed. The picture you hold in your mind influences and impacts every area of your life. I've experienced a completely new life since implementing these practices, and everything for me has changed. My finances, my health, my spiritual life, my relationships, my skills, and my abilities. Everything.

Think about the benefits of having a clear, concise vision.

☐ Vision gives you fulfillment.

Many women contend with the annoyance of, I wonder, if only, and what if. *"What if I would have tried … I wonder what I could accomplish if I dared to …. If only I had taken that risk, I wonder if it's too late …"* A life filled with what-ifs can only lead to regret. And oh, how painful is regret? However, when you purpose in your heart to awaken your God-dream and cultivate your life's purpose and vision, you will experience deep satisfaction and fulfillment. You can savor the thrill of victory, delivered from the agony of defeat. (Remember ABC's *Wide World of Sports?*)

☐ Vision puts you in charge of your life.

You are the co-creator of your life. Becoming a bravehearted woman means accepting the responsibility and privilege of designing the life you believe God has called you to live. I know dreaming takes faith and determination. Still, if you don't set your vision, intentions, and agenda for your life, someone else will. And guess what they have planned for you? Not much. So, don't acquiesce, my sister. Be brave and live your best life.

☐ Vision mutes distractions.

Life is loud. Everyone wants our attention. Social media intrudes into every nook and cranny of our life, and even our most intimate moments are distracted by our phones. There is no shortage of annoying voices vying for our focus. But piercing through the daily bombilating razzamatazz comes the clarion call of your compelling vision, muting the distractions. You will know what voice to listen to when vision is in charge of your life.

☐ Vision saves you time, money, and energy.

Say goodbye to indecision. With vision, you're sure about your priorities, and your focus is well-defined. You know when to say yes or no. That clarity is a beautiful thing. You won't be drained at the end of every day, feeling frustrated because you once again neglected yourself and the list you had hoped to accomplish. Vision drives you to live intentionally. No more squandered energy. You make the most of your time.

☐ Vision gives juice to wake up in the morning.

When a powerful and clear picture of your desired future energizes you, you wake up each day excited to achieve your dreams and goals. Some mornings, I want to hit the snooze button, roll over, and grab ten more minutes of sleep, but then I imagine my plan for the day, which always includes something to move me closer to my goals. In seconds, I'm eager to get going and conquer my day. What happened? Slumber gave way to desire. Vision gave me vitality.

☐ Vision imposes discipline.

Another fantastic by-product of vision is the discipline you gain. When your dream is crystal clear, concise, and compelling, and you desire it with all your heart, you'll find a fresh determination and solid commitment to doing whatever it takes to meet your goals. Here's an easy example: Let's say you have a goal of shedding 25 lbs. before your daughter's wedding. Use your God-given imagination (more on imagination in the pages ahead) to envision yourself weighing your ideal weight, with arms toned and skin glowing. Not only see this vivid picture in your mind, *but feel it.* The joy and confidence you radiate as you greet your guests are palatable. Can you see the image of you in your slender and beautifully fit dress? Can you sense the pleasure as you dance the night away? Once you have a vision so alive inside you, you'll activate a new discipline. When someone offers you French fries, pizza, or dessert, you'll quickly and decisively say, "No, thank you." That choice doesn't align with your vision. You only desire what brings you closer to your dreams. That's the incredible force of vision.

Where there is no vision, people throw off focus.

—My paraphrase. Proverbs 29:18

What is Your Vision?

*The bravest are surely those who have the clearest vision
of what is before them, glory and danger alike, and yet
notwithstanding, go out to meet it.*

—Thucydides

So, BraveHeart, what is your vision? Do you know what you want **in** life and **from** life? Are you convinced of your purpose, calling, and reason for being on this earth? Can you clearly articulate what you want, and if so, do you have it written on paper? Do you look at your vision every day? Are you thanking God in advance for what you can see in your mind, though perhaps, not yet in your hands? And do you have clearly defined goals with a plan of action to get you there? Don't worry if you cannot answer yes to any or all these queries. I'm simply posing questions to stir you to think about what you should think about. I want you to get curious about your life so you can see what's possible.

And understand, whether or not you know it, you're living a vision right now. You're being guided either by an idea you have intentionally designed or directed and motivated by the image of your unconscious mind, intent on keeping you safe, comfortable, and securely out of the reach of change.

Is Yours a Life of Design or Default?

As I mentioned above, just because you're unaware of a vision for your life doesn't mean there isn't one. There is. It's called the vision of default.

Without an intentionally designed, blueprint, your unconscious mind has gone to work and created the plan for you, drawing from the databank filled and available to your brain. Childhood experiences, traumas, past pain, spiritual beliefs, current trends, peer pressures, cultural expectations, parental values, and more are the resources in the databank stored in your unconscious memory.

When the default system is constructing the plan for your life, here's what you'll get:

◊ An average lifestyle with a few accidental good breaks.

◊ Stuck in ruts. Living the same ole' life for years.

◊ Dealing with the same problems with no progress toward healthy solutions.

◊ Chronic financial instability.

◊ Unsustainable quality of life. Many ups and downs.

◊ Numerous failures and do-overs.

◊ Many starts but no follow-through to completion.

◊   End up in a dead-end life you don't enjoy.

◊   Struggling relationships.

◊   Disempowerment and unhappiness.

◊   Negative emotions such as lostness, confusion, invisibility, and unworthiness.

◊   Unfulfilled dreams.

◊   Ultimately, lots of regrets!

Did you see yourself in more than three of these areas? Don't despair, but be aware. If you are still looking for a clear-cut vision and if it's challenging to take brave action steps to accomplish your goal, then you're probably stuck. You won't live the fulfilled life God wants you to have. You're living by default. Why not fire up your imagination instead? Get your journal, find a quiet and soothing space, and invite God to give you his inspired ideas and dreams for your life. It only takes a spark to get your fire going.

Ignite Your Imagination

An excellent and playful scene in the movie *Hook*, starring Robin Williams, demonstrates an important point for us bravehearted dreamers. Let me set it up for you. Middle-aged and somewhat fluffy-framed Peter Banning (Robin Williams) has long since left his magical childhood in Neverland. Now he's an average family man with an average career as an average attorney, experiencing less-than-average contentment. Suddenly, average is interrupted when a drastic turn of events forces Peter Banning to return to the enchanted Neverland of his youth. In one scene, Peter sits bellied up at a dinner table (with no food) surrounded by his former band of brothers, the Lost Boys of Neverland, and his best friend, Tinkerbell. The scene unfolds, revealing a sad truth; Peter has abandoned his imagination and can no longer dream, invent, or, the tragedy of all tragedies, fly. Peter's memory of his true identity—Peter Pan—is foggy at best and, at worst, buried deep in the recesses of his subconscious mind. Unfortunately, without the re-ignition of his imagination, Peter will never re-capture the essence of who he is. He will never dream again. He will never soar. As they sit around the empty table, waiting for food to manifest, an argument of epic insult breaks out between the former leader, Peter, and the new leader of the Lost Boys gang, Rufio. Peter wins the skirmish and, in a display of victory, picks up his spoon, scoops an *imaginary* gob of gooey soup, and hurls it toward Rufio. What happens next shocks Peter and delights the Lost Boys. Bright-colored goo splatters Rufio's face. Peter sits frozen, inspecting the food-coated spoon, when Lost Boy, named Pockets, whispers in his ear, "You're doing it, Peter."

"Doing what?"

"You're using your imagination."

Instantly, the table is bursting with colorful and delectable food, made visible by the re-birth of Peter's imagination. He had come alive. [11]

The point is vividly clear. As adults, we have forsaken our childlike faith and abandoned our wild and fantastical imaginations. No longer do we dream. We have encountered disappointments and find it too painful to hope again. Instead, we've accepted average as our lot in life and settled for false contentment. We've placed limits on what we'll believe and shoved a lid on the well-spring of our bubbling imagination. If that's you, I want to embolden you—give yourself permission to dream again. Take the limits off, remove the lid, and decide today that you won't settle for average. In my course BraveHearted YOUniversity, (https://www. braveheartedwoman.com/braveheart-youniversity) I invite the women I'm coaching to re-ignite their imaginations.

We start by finding a quiet place, somewhere beautiful that incites creativity, along with a journal and a pen with which we love to write.

Then I offer writing prompts and instruct the students to let their imaginations flow unedited.

"Write something that scares you, that feels so big it seems impossible," I tell them. "Picture where you would like to travel, what kind of home you want, what movie you would like to write and produce, a book you want to write, or business you want to buy." The goal is to stretch their imagination muscle and awaken dormant dreams.

That's what I want for you, too. I'm here to motivate your heart to dream again. Use the gift of imagination to get a picture of the mind-blowing marvels God has created for you to have and experience. Sit quietly and allow your soul to explore freely. Don't interrupt, judge, or censor your dream. Unleash your mind to dream, and with spiritual eyes, see what you can't yet see in the natural world. Your vision may come in small pieces, glimpses, or fragments of images. Those snapshots mean the rekindling of your fire within—your imagination is working. Then, take time to write—are you ready for this—no less than 50 images you'd like to see, do, experience, buy, or have in your future. The same rules apply; No judgment, editing, or interrupting your dreaming. Just let the pen flow on the paper. Study after study shows even the process of putting pen to paper engages the creative side of your brain and increases your ability to imagine. So, imagine big, bold, and brave.

You Create What You See

Author Terri Savelle often says, "If you see nothing, you can expect nothing." Yikes! The thought of nothing frightens me. I always want the God dream burning inside my heart and mind. Captivated. I've learned whatever I see consciously or unconsciously, I create. That's true for you too. Whether your vision is positive and beautiful or negative and undesirable, you will draw to yourself precisely what you think about and visualize.

What image do you hold in your mind? The clearer your vision, the easier it is to obtain. Be specific and write every detail. For example, does your vision include you living on the water? If so, is it the ocean or a lake? Where are you? Is it some place warm and tropical like Florida? Or are you dreaming of a cabin in the woods on the water in Northern Michigan?

Maybe your vision is to travel. Where do you want to go? Are you dreaming of a trip to Venice, Italy? Will you stay in a villa? Will you ride down the Venice Canal in a gondola? Or do you envision your ideal travels to take you to the snowy mountains of Denver, Colorado? If you only say, "I want to travel," your vision is too vague, with no exact target. Your brain is uncertain, so you can expect vague, ambiguous results.

You must *see* it before you can *see* it. You have to see your vision twice, first in your mind with your spiritual vision and then a second time with your natural eyes when your dream becomes a reality. Here's a principle I enjoy teaching my clients: you must see, smell, taste, and feel your vision right down to the last detail. However, occasionally, someone will ask, "Do I have to have a specific vision? Can't I flow from one day to the next? I'm more of a take-it-as-it-comes kind of person." Maybe you've wanted to ask that, too. Well, those are good questions, and I understand the principle of taking "one day at a time." But don't let that laid-back, Que sera sera, do-nothing philosophy trick you into living without an intentional focus. Without a vision for your desired future and a plan to get you there, your soul will wither and die. Unfortunately, I've seen it happen. Too many women deteriorate, especially in midlife.

God created *you* to contain fire, remember? Not a brush fire that's burning today and fizzled out tomorrow. No, your Creator wants you to possess an ever-present glow of burning coals, and that's precisely what a clear vision will do for you in every season of your life. So, to answer those questions with a resounding *yes*, you must have a dream. Vision is where your best life begins.

People perish without a vision!

Don't Perish Before You Die

The biggest reason midlife women arrive at the second half of life with regret, fear, sadness, grief, depression, lostness, and confusion is they can only see themselves in the present and the past. They *see* themselves slipping away. Their youth is fleeing, no matter how desperately they try to preserve the vitality of days gone by. The problem? They have no picture, no vision for their next chapter of life. And what these women see in their minds is scary: images of decrepit, frail older women. No wonder unhappiness assails so many women at this crossroads in life. That picture is enough to make anyone cringe.

I once heard a pastor say vision is God's solution for the disappointed, downcast, discouraged, distracted, and defeated.

If your life is missing something or if you're disappointed, downcast, discouraged, distracted, defeated, or disenchanted, you most likely lack vision.

You don't have to live with that despair, wondering what to do with your life. You don't have to fill your schedule with busyness or daily living with no focus, motivation, or courage to change your circumstances.

You are a bravehearted woman with a fresh vision on the horizon. You expect more of your life than what you can currently see. You're willing to dare to hope for something beyond your wildest imagination.

Walk bravely, reach, believe, adjust, evaluate, plan, and prioritize. Then, you're on your way.

> *We are not limited by our abilities but by our*
> *lack of vision.*
>
> —Dawn Damon

Brave Challenge #5: Dream

Find a quiet and inspiring place to reflect, free from interruptions. Turn off your phone. Grab a journal and a free-flowing pen or pencil. Write no less than 50 images you'd like to see, do, experience, buy, or have in your future. Let your imagination run free. Don't judge, edit, or interrupt your soul from dreaming. Allow the pen to flow on the paper. Imagine big.

Chapter Seven

Fortitude 2: Cultivate a Real Identity.
I Believe

The greater danger for most of us lies not in setting our aim to high and falling short; but in setting our aim too low and achieving our mark.

—Michelangelo

You're here, on Earth, for a purpose. A grand and thrilling purpose. The question is, do you believe that to be true? Do you believe you're the woman God calls to live an extraordinary life *and* your best and most significant years of life are still ahead of you? If this idea scares you yet inspires a bit of hope, you're on your way to cultivating Fortitude number two—an authentic, real identity.

In the last chapter, I asked you to sit quietly and reflect on the vision you desire for your life. How did you do?

Did your dreams come quickly, or did you sit with a blank page before you? Were you able to let your imagination pioneer into uncharted territory, or did you play it safe and write what seemed doable and, dare I say, even average? Did you set your aim too low?

If your dreams don't scare you or even seem outlandish, you're not dreaming big enough. I'm not saying your vision should be unrealizable and foolish. But as one person said when repeating what God spoke to their heart, "Ask me for something that lets me know I'm God."

When did you last ask God for something so big it made you shiver? Well, get ready. As a bravehearted woman, you will learn to assert your faith.

Do You Suffer from F.I.B.S?

On my bathroom mirror, I have scripted in crayon the letters G.H.B.P. That stands for "God Honors Bold Prayers." I've scribbled those letters with childlike faith to remind me to ask God boldly. God truly delights in big dreams, brave faith, and bold visions.

Since we know this is the case, what stops us from taking leaps of faith and aiming big? There's at least one culprit behind our low aim.

What is it?

False identity.

I call it F.I.B.S. - False Identity Belief Syndrome.

We falsely believe we're not worthy or capable of living a spectacular life. Lies, limits, and labels tell us we are not good enough, smart enough, young enough, rich enough, or any other "I'm not something enough." As a result of F.I.B.S., we shrink our vision to match those lies. Whether conscious or unconscious, we live the life we think we are worth. If we can't see ourselves living a great life with success, earning a sizable income, and enjoying beautiful relationships, then we won't live an exceptional life, find success, or have healthy relationships. It's like trying to live a million-dollar life with a scratch-and-dent price tag hanging on us.

In the mid-1800s, Soren Kierkegaard, a Danish philosopher, wrote a parable about a pair of thieves who broke into a jewelry store and did something very strange. Instead of stealing priceless jewels, these two robbers played a prank. They switched all the price tags. Taking the high-priced tags off the expensive jewelry, they put them on the costume jewelry. Then they took the bargain price tags off the costume jewelry and placed them on the costly and rare pieces.

As usual, the jewelry store opened for business the following day, but no one noticed what the thieves had done. For the next several weeks, folks purchased $10,000 rings for only a few dollars, and others bought $9 necklaces for thousands. [12]

That story describes it well. You're priceless, but the thief wants to label you as dollar-store goods.

You can never outperform your own self-image.

—Dr. Maxwell Maltz

So, let's dive into Fortitude number two because understanding and claiming an identity worth all the beauty and greatness God has in store for you is your right, but also your choice—and the essence of living full out. You *are* the woman God calls and has plans for. Big. Brave. Bold and excellent plans. Why don't you take a step of faith right now and write this on your mirror; G.H.B.B.B.D.

God Honors Big, Bold, Brave Dreams.

What Identity Will You Choose?

Psychologists define identity as an individual's sense of self, the qualities, personality traits, beliefs, appearance, and expressions that characterize their sense of self, and how they believe others perceive them.

You may not have thought much about your identity, but it affects every area of your life. As a bravehearted woman with everything to offer the world, you need to know if the image you hold of yourself propels you forward or holds you back.

To learn this, require of yourself an exploration of *you*. Make yourself answer these probing questions:

◊ Who am I?

◊ What do I like?

◊ What motivates me?

◊ What are my passions and core values?

◊ What triggers me and makes me angry?

◊ What am I good at doing—my talents, skills, and abilities?

◊ What personality traits do I possess?

You have a unique fingerprint to leave on this world. Learn to know what it is and how you contribute.

Women who answer these questions with clarity have a sense of self and benefit immensely from knowing who they are. I want that for you because everything flows from a bravehearted identity; confidence, sound decision-making, security, flourishing relationships, fulfillment and purpose, bolstered self-worth, and a life of joy and authenticity.

No wonder Socrates said, "Man Know Thyself." (Or, in our case, Woman Know Thyself!)

But, as you'll see in a moment, "knowing yourself" is just the tip of the iceberg. You're so much more than what you know.

Three Parts of Your Identity

To wholly know thyself, you must understand the three parts that make up your identity.

1.   Your Created Image

God created you to look like him. He infused his likeness into your being. Simply put, you're sheer genius, brilliant beyond description. The Psalmist David said, "I have been remarkably and wonderfully made" (Psalm 139:14 HCSB). In essence, David said, "I'm incredibly awesome because of you, God. You surpassed all expectations and made me extraordinary" (My paraphrase. See Psalm 139:14). What made King David make such a bold, brave assertion? Undoubtedly, he received a revelation of his intrinsic value and worth. God masterfully made him. When David honored the value of himself, he honored God.

Have you received the same revelation? Can you declare, "I am one remarkable woman? In fact, I'm flat-out breathtaking. Look how God created me—outstanding."

Now, don't try this in public for the first time—you may get a few odd looks—but if you've never said those words to yourself, get up and go to the nearest mirror, look yourself in the eyes, and tell yourself, "Guurrrl, you're straight-up amazing." Make that declaration. Not because of anything you've done to earn it, but because God created you to bear his image.

Drop the mic here.

Today, will you choose, by faith (not feelings) the truth of your created identity? Honor the God-created woman you are—wonderfully and fearfully made.

> *Do you want to meet the love of your life? Look in the mirror!*
>
> —Byron Katie

2.   Your Redemptive Image

Your jaw will drop when you consider how divinely intricate you've been made. The dignity God created you to possess is awe-inspiring. Yet, I can hear the soul-dissonance of every woman who says, "But you don't know what I've done. God may have made me beautiful, but I no longer carry that pure and glorious image. I've made too many mistakes and bad decisions. My head knows I'm not disqualified from accepting the honor of being God's image-bearer, but in my heart, I don't measure up to the standard."

I know the pain of those words because I've spoken them about myself. I've suffered shame and disappointment myself for not being good enough. *How can a flawed, wrecked, and broken woman reflect a holy God?* I've also coached hundreds of women who whispered in vulnerable moments of self-reflection, "If I'm so wonderful, why do I feel so unworthy?"

If you're a woman of faith, you know the answer to the question that echoes from the cavern of damaged self-worth. Unworthiness is the result of sin. It has destroyed your original God-design. And although your core worth and value are undeniable, sin ravaged your soul and left you (and me) for dead.

But *you*, my bravehearted sister, were to die for. Even in your pillaged state, Jesus salvaged you. He redeemed you—rescued, reclaimed, and ransomed you—by giving his life in exchange for yours.

When I was a young girl, I adored spending summer vacations with my grandparents on their farm in Indiana. There, with Grandpa, my two sisters, and my cousins, I developed a fascinating love for scavenger hunting—a whimsical pleasure I enjoy today. Grandpa would rumble up in his big red truck, roll down the window, and holler to us kids playing in the pasture, "Who wants to go to the junkyard?" Then, piling into the 1950s Chevy truck, we were off to the dump. But for me, it was treasure-seeking. Mounds and mounds of bottles, trinkets, and other unwanted goods, discarded as junk to one person, were priceless gems with potential to us kids. After finding the object we wanted to rescue, we happily scrambled back into Grandpa's Chevy, securing our newfound beauty.

Although very inadequate, my story exemplifies what Jesus did for you. He redeemed you from sin and paid the price to set you free so you could return to the beautiful treasure God created.

So, why tell you all this? Because it's crucial you recognize the second truth about your identity. You were created with inherent value, but when sin marred God's original design, Jesus exchanged his life for yours, giving you a "redemptive identity." By saying yes to Jesus as your Savior, you're restored and given an ah-maz-ing identity in Christ. Again, this identity is your reality, whether or not you agree it's true. God gives you the gift of a new image, which is precisely how he sees you.

Read in the first person what God's Word says about you:

- ◊ I am chosen.
- ◊ I am valuable.
- ◊ I am accepted.
- ◊ I am loved.
- ◊ I am made worthy.
- ◊ I am adequate.
- ◊ I am brave.
- ◊ I am competent.
- ◊ I am complete.
- ◊ I am holy.
- ◊ I am blameless.
- ◊ I am purified.
- ◊ I am forgiven.
- ◊ I am a new creation.
- ◊ I am God's design.
- ◊ I am washed clean.
- ◊ I am free from guilt.
- ◊ I am God's delight.

◊   I am an overcomer.

◊   I am free.

◊   I can do all things.

◊   I am a warrior.

That's you, bravehearted woman. I told you. You are amazing.

Choose to accept this identity. Wear it like a new dress.

3.   Your Self-Image

*Everything in your life is the product of the identity you
have accepted to be true of yourself.*

—David Ramos

Now that we've laid the foundation for your true God-given identity. Let's look at your identity through another lens—how you see yourself.

You have an opinion about yourself and it dictates your life's quality.

Whether or note you know it, you've been gathering evidence about yourself since your early childhood. Influencers, such as parents, caregivers, teachers, siblings, coaches, friends, and other significant people, have treated you in ways, which have provided evidence. Add in words and labels spoken over you and your early life experiences, and you'll understand how you came to view yourself.

You've constructed a self-image based on beliefs about yourself and what you think you deserve and can expect from life.

To further support that self-construct, you've unconsciously compiled a mental dictionary filled with words and descriptions that apply to you.

If your self-assessment is healthy, your dictionary will offer words like capable, beautiful, talented, tenacious, exceptional, attractive, strong, and more.

But, if your formative years were hard and unpleasant, your self-image probably took a significant hit. In that case, your internal dictionary gives you words such as inadequate, unlovable, damaged, fat, stupid, misfit, and other denigrations.

What identity have you accepted to be true for you?

You must recognize the lens through which you view and appraise yourself. Because your collection of beliefs informs how you live.

Many women accept their created and redemptive identity. That's great. But I've met too many women with discord between what they biblically agree is true about their identity and what they *feel* is true. In these cases, women have hidden and deeply buried false beliefs, F.I.B.S., operating in their unconscious mind, perpetuating negative thoughts, feelings, behaviors, and, ultimately, very low self-worth. And on top of accepting a low opinion of themselves, they add a heap full of shame and guilt for feeling bad about themselves when they know they *should* be walking in faith and victory.

In my healing and recovery process from childhood sexual trauma, I experienced this same dichotomy. I wanted to live confidently, believing in my value, so I believed God's truest words about me were exactly what God said. But I also had nagging and relentless fears about my worth. At times—and I'm exaggerating a bit—I needed to earn my right to *even* breathe and prove I was valuable. Unbeknown to me, lies repressed in my unconscious mind produced doubts about my self-worth. I compensated with works, striving for acceptance and approval.

What about you?

How do you truly see yourself? What's the story you tell yourself about yourself? Is your narration positive, powerful, and filled with faith and vision, or are you using words from a faulty internal dictionary laden with victim vocabulary to tell your story? You may be accepting F.I.B.S.

You cannot outperform or rise above the level of your self-image, but once you know your true worth, you will soar.

So, get ready to shed that old identity. Choose to change the price tag you've been wearing and mark yourself up. Only you can raise the appraised value you've placed on yourself.

Identity is this incredible invisible force that controls your whole life. It's invisible like gravity is invisible, but it controls your whole life.

—Tony Robbins

Woman Unknow Thyself

We know who we are, but not who we may become.

—William Shakespeare

Earlier, I said you need to know thyself to take an honest inventory of who you are, what you like, and where you're gifted and talented. Now I'm going to tell you something that may surprise you. To really discover, grow, and build your authentic identity, you have to be willing to *unknow yourself.*

Part of the sanctification process of the Holy Spirit is to strip away the false constructs we have accumulated and enable our true selves to emerge.

—Peter Scazzero [13]

Unknowing yourself retrieves the God-image you were designed to reflect.

It's the unraveling of Lazarus' grave clothes to set the real you free. It's the chipping of marble to reveal the angel. As Michelangelo said, "I saw the angel in the marble and carved until I set (her) free." It's the fig leaves upon Eve, covering her true beauty. It's the editor who eliminates excess, so the beauty of the story appears more poignant.

When you unknow what you *think* is true of you, you surrender to the divine sculptor who sets the true you free.

When you *unknow* what you've always assumed is true, you unleash curiosity about yourself, your potential, and your passions. You question what keeps you from evolving into the woman you long to be. You ignore fear and allow the unwrapping of false, self-protective coverings. You become vulnerable so you can reunite with your true self.

> *More often than not, finding out what you love doing most is about recovering an old love or an inescapable truth that has been silenced for years, even decades. When you come to your dream job, your thing, it is rarely a first encounter. It's usually a reunion.*
>
> —Jonathan Acuff [14]

Ask yourself if you're ready and willing to relinquish the distorted and negative labels you've used to define yourself. Are you prepared to surrender, the beliefs that seem harmless enough yet still entangle you in mediocrity and thwart your growth. Do you want to throw off that thieving price tag and own your true worth?

If you answered yes just now, this is an exciting and liberating moment. The renewal process is a soul metamorphosis. God's word refers to unknowing yourself as "putting off and putting on."

"You were taught, with regard to your former way of life, to put off your old self, which is being corrupted by its deceitful desires; to be made new in the attitude of your minds, and to put on the new self, created to be like God in true righteousness and holiness" (Ephesian 4:22-24 NIV).

It's our choice to put on the new self, to live into an identity that carries all the attributes and authority God has designed and delegated to us.

Here's how you can participate in the process of putting off and putting on to be made new in the attitude of your mind.

Five Ways to Unknow Thyself

◊ Question.

In unknowing yourself, you carefully listen to your narrative and question your assessments and conclusions about yourself. Ask, "Is that thought really true?" Put off any thought or idea that doesn't align with your God-given identity.

◊ Challenge.

Put off negative assumptions about your:

◊ Identity: Stop saying, "I am not something enough."

◊ Ability: Stop saying, "I don't have what I need. I'm not able."

◊ Validity: Stop saying, "I'm not deserving or worthy. I don't qualify."

◊ Capability: Stop saying, "I don't have what it takes. I'm not capable."

◊ **Surrender.**

Put off your loyalty to any thoughts of average, smallness, or woeful inadequacy you think you have. Place it all on the chopping block.

◊ **Rewrite.**

Put off all the "rules" you have written for yourself about yourself and grant yourself permission to rewrite the script.

◊ **Renew.**

Put off the old mind. Let the Holy Spirit strip away your former thinking and replace it with the truth. In this way, you put on a new mind.

Sculpt Your Identity

I always wanted to be someone. I see now I should have been more specific.

—Lilly Tomlin

Finally, choose how you want to sculpt your identity. Be specific. Take control. Chip away what doesn't serve you well. You decide who and what will shape your self-image. Others have been feeding your self-worth, but not anymore. You're the molder of your identity. Be careful how you construct it, and always be willing to learn, grow, and improve. Remove the excess.

Crafting a new identity always requires courage, but if you catch even a tiny glimpse of who you are created to be, you'll have the motivation to become her. She's within you.

Dare to believe and live into your highest purpose.

You have one life to live, so make the mark only you can make.

I was privileged to hear author, entrepreneur, and High-Performance Coach Ed Mylett speak at a conference I attended. His words struck me when he said, "I have this weird version of heaven. When I show up there, I get to meet the man I was destined to become. This is the best version of me. He's the man who lived full out, kept his commitments, and wrote the books. When I meet him, we're twins. I'll say, dude, I've been chasing you my whole life! And hell would be meeting the man I was destined to become and finding out we are complete strangers."

Don't be a stranger to the woman God intended you to become.

Brave Challenge #6: Sculpt

James Clear says, *"You can decide what kind of person you want to be."* Deeply reflect on these questions and start sculpting.

◊   Who do you want to be?

◊   What values do you want to stand for?

◊   What principles are important to you?

◊   What traits and characteristics do you want to be known for?

◊   Who is the type of person who can achieve the outcomes you want?

◊   Where are you being called to show up as the person you most want to be?

Take the Challenge to Strengthen Your Identity:

https://www.braveheartedwoman.com/identity-challenge-ebook

Chapter Eight

Fortitude 3: Choose an Able Mindset.
I Think

*Be careful how you think; your life is shaped by
your thoughts.*

—Proverbs 4:23 GNT

I could end this chapter right here. Your thoughts shape your life. Said another way, how you think determines who you are, what you do, and the quality of the life you will live. Of all the Five Fortitudes, choosing a bravehearted mindset ranks as one of the highest.

That's because thoughts create reality—what you think about, you bring about. Your thoughts produce results. Your mind is that powerful.

With the mind, people can think themselves into sickness or health, well-being or depression, anxiety or peace, doubt or confidence. In fact, your current life is the sum of how you think and what you believe.

If you want to build a better life, you must start with better thoughts. Managing your thought life, therefore, is critical to your success. Your mindset is the architect of your future.

In this chapter, I want you to consider how you think, not your fleeting thoughts alone, but "thought habits," which, over time, create mindsets that create outcomes.

I define a mindset as a cluster of established and habitual beliefs, opinions, and attitudes a person holds and forms over time. Most often, your mindsets operate without conscious awareness—like cruise control on your car. With intentionality, you can raise your awareness and discover the beliefs and attitudes you possess that comprise your mindsets and how those mindsets drive your life.

Pause. Ponder. Pick.

Be empowered. You can decide the thoughts you want to accept.

In reading the Bible this past week, I found a verse in *The Passion Translation* that stopped me in my tracks. It read, "… stop having the mindset of a slave" (1 Corinthians 7:23b TPT).

The apostle Paul tells the people to *stop the mindset* that was controlling them. This verse infers that the people should not only stop their slave mentality but also choose a new, better, more powerful mindset.

As a bravehearted woman, you choose the mindsets that will propel you to success and victory. Just because a thought comes to you does not mean you have to accept it, fellowship with it, or believe it. You have the power and the responsibility to examine your thoughts and decide what you want to do with them. Do you want to accept the thought? Reject it? Replace it? Reframe it?

Thinking through this decision is the process I call Pause, Ponder, and Pick.

Pause

When a thought or series of thoughts come to you about a situation, your life circumstances, or your relationships, hit the pause button and suspend that thought. To instantly pause your thoughts, change your physiology. Stand up, clap your hands, change your posture, smile, speak out loud, sing, or execute any other physical movement interrupting your train of thought. Pausing quickly leads you to the next step.

Ponder

Think about your thoughts. Reflect and ask questions such as:

◊   Is this thought true?

◊   Is this thought honorable, right, and pure?

◊   Does this thought serve me well, or does it drag me down?

◊   Does this thought come from a positive mindset or a negative one?

When you've discovered the nature of your thoughts and how they will affect you, it's time to *pick*.

Pick

What do you want to do with your thoughts? Do you want to meditate on them? Or examine your thoughts and see if they pass the Philippians 4:8 test, "Finally, brothers and sisters, whatever is true, whatever is noble, whatever is right, whatever is pure, whatever is lovely, whatever is admirable—if anything is excellent or praiseworthy—think about such things" (NIV).

Or do you need to cast those thoughts down and replace them with more empowering thoughts?

You get to pick.

Using these three steps allows you to take control of your mind and safeguard it against the onslaught of damaging mindsets. At first, Pause, Ponder, and Pick will feel mechanical, maybe even awkward, but the more you practice it, the more natural and automatic it will become. You'll fortify your mind and become a tremendous gatekeeper for yourself.

Every thought produces emotions and feelings. So, pay attention to your mood. If you're feeling anxious, depressed, sad, or some other intense emotion, it's possible you didn't catch yourself amid negative thinking, and some sneaky thoughts have slipped in undetected and under the radar, perhaps even in the unconscious mind.

In that case, ask yourself—with journal and pen in hand—why am I feeling sad, anxious, irritated? Name the emotion as specifically as you can. Was there a precipitating event or meditation of thought you can recall?

I do this routine often. Once in a while, because of past trauma, I'll experience a *trigger*, an emotional response to an event, memory, or some other sensory reminder. When this happens, I know something has dysregulated my peaceful state. So, I grab my journal, sit quietly, and pray as the Psalmist David did, "Why, my soul, are you downcast? Why so disturbed within me?" Then I wait for an answer and journal the impressions I'm sensing, thoughts and feelings that align with scripture and almost always bring my soul peace and clarity.

This process—pause, ponder, and pick—is how we stay integrated and connected to what's happening in our body, soul, and spirit. When we're aware of how we think and feel, we guard our hearts and protect ourselves from a hostile takeover from thoughts and feelings. Pausing helps us choose a positive *response* to life's events and not simply *react*.

So above all, guard the affections of your heart, for they affect all that you are. Pay attention to the welfare of your innermost being, for from there flows the wellspring of life"

—Proverbs 4:23 TPT

Choose Your Mindset

"The only person you're destined to become is the person you decide to be."

—Ralph Waldo Emmerson

I'll say it again. Your thoughts are driving your life. The good news is you can choose what you want to dwell on and, as a result, choose the direction you want your life to head.

Pastor of Life Church Craig Groeschel said, *"Your life is constantly moving in the direction of your strongest thought."*

Do you know what you're choosing as your most prominent thoughts? You can't live a positive life with negative thoughts. Suppose your thoughts are primarily negative, with scary images, scenarios of defeat and embarrassment, unforgiveness, bitterness, and jealousy. In that case, your life will move toward more bitterness and defeat. But if your thoughts are good and uplifting, resourceful, and full of optimism and faith, you can expect your life to move in the direction of success and joy!

Proverbs 23:7 gives us this wisdom: "For as he thinketh in his heart, so is he" (KJV). This biblical picture shows a rich ruler who says one thing with his words but thinks another in his heart. His words and thoughts are not aligned. That man is more authentically how he *thinks* than what he *says*.

Since my life is constantly moving in the direction of my most prominent thought and image, I hold powerful and beautiful images in my mind's eye. I see myself overcoming, succeeding, creating, and accomplishing. I see myself at the perfect weight, toned, strong, and healthy. I envision myself signing copies of my best-selling books. I picture myself speaking on stage and blessing audiences with the messages God gives me.

Vanity?

Not at all.

I'm picturing the person God says I am. I'm choosing life and imagining where I want my life to head. I align my words, actions, and affirmations with the vision I hold in my heart.

Now it's your turn.

In the coming paragraphs, I will outline the seven mindsets you must choose and cultivate to live a bravehearted life. I call them the Seven G-Fierce Mindsets! (*Yes, another coined term.*)

◊   The Growth Mindset

◊   The Grateful Mindset

◊   The Genius Mindset

◊   The Gritty Mindset

◊   The Generous Mindset

◊   The Gaining Edge Mindset

◊   The Genuine Mindset

These paradigm shifts can completely transform you. You'll experience change in every area of your life.

So, let's get our shift together! Whaddya say?

Growth Mindset

A growth mindset means you believe you can grow, learn, improve, and change. It means you think your intelligence, skills, and abilities are malleable and not set in stone. A growth mindset enables you to expand, develop, and evolve through effort, practice, and resilience. You view the brain as a muscle to develop and improve through practice and repetition. With a growth mindset, you consider that anything is possible.

The opposite mindset is called a fixed mindset, which believes intelligence, abilities, and capacity to grow are fixed, etched in stone, and inflexible. A fixed mindset argues "no amount of effort or practice can change me. I am who I am, and that's it." People with a fixed mindset avoid challenges, lack resilience, and feel threatened by the success of others.

As a coach, it takes little time to determine whether my client adheres to a growth or fixed mindset. If she rises brave, invigorated by new challenges, invites and welcomes feedback, and thrives while tackling hard stuff, I know she believes she can grow and change.

If, however, I offer a challenge or present feedback and my client feels anxious, ashamed, and demotivated by "all the pressure," I'm reasonably sure she already views herself as defeated and feels she will inevitably fail. Observing my clients' attitudes about difficulties or when faced with challenges always gives me a good benchmark of their current belief system.

This phenomenon is what Psychologist Carol Dweck noticed more than 30 years ago while working with students. Her research specialized in motivation and how students dealt with failure. Carol and her colleagues recognized that some students easily and quickly rebounded after setbacks and failures. In contrast, disappointment derailed other students who were devastated by even the smallest failures. To describe the fundamental beliefs people have about their intelligence, how they view challenges, obstacles, criticisms, and the success of others, Dr. Dweck named her findings the "Fixed and Growth Mindsets."

Gwen's story helps us understand the growth mindset vs. a fixed mindset.

Gwen is a midlife woman who regrets she never finished her degree. Through the prompting of her daughter, Gwen agreed to pursue a certification in an area of her interest. To join the next semester of training, Gwen must take an entrance exam to measure the level of her current skill set. On the day of her exam, Gwen was nervous and had difficulty answering some questions. Gwen completed the test but worried she didn't pass. Was this idea was even worth her time?

The test results arrived in her email the next day, and she realized her worst fears. Although she was very close—in fact, closer than she thought—Gwen did not pass. The school, offered her an opportunity for tutoring and a test retake in a few months.

How do you imagine Gwen will respond? See if you can identify which thoughts come from a fixed mindset and which ones come from a growth mindset.

1. I did better than I thought, and with more study and practice, I can ace this test.
2. I guess I don't have what it takes to get certified. I'm just not smart enough. It was a dumb idea, anyway.
3. I'm no good at math; I've never been and never will. I feel like such a failure. I quit.
4. With the help of a tutor, I can get better at those math problems. I love a good challenge. I'll be ready for sure in a couple of months!

Did you see it?

Did you feel it? The despair and defeatism in examples 2 and 3 are palpable.

With this fixed and negative mindset, it's no wonder Gwen didn't finish school and needed her daughter to coax her to take a courageous step. That failure mindset is driving her life right into the ditch.

What did you notice about answers 1 and 4? Did you sense a positive attitude? Gwen was upbeat and incredibly resilient. She embraced the challenge and didn't view herself as a failure. Gwen didn't fold up and quit. Instead, she offered herself a healthy pep talk and declared victory. She accepted the daunting challenge from her daughter to sign up, and with the advice provided by the school, she said yes to the tutor and the test retake. A growth mindset propelled Gwen into success and elevated her life.

Which Gwen are you?

I have to admit I've been both kinds of Gwen. I've stared challenges in the face and said, "Get outta my way; I'm coming through."And I've also tucked my tail and cowered in the corner. But in every situation, I'm still response-able. I choose my mindset, and you do too.

Why not choose a Growth Mindset and adopt this frame of mind as a perpetual and consistent way to think? As a bravehearted woman with Growth Mindset, your life will blossom and flourish.

The Grateful Mindset

Gratitude is the best lens through which to view your life.

If you decide on a mindset of gratitude, and I trust you will, you will catapult your life into joy and happiness. You simply can't be bitter and grateful at the same time. Gratitude destroys the toxic emotions that will otherwise drain energy and motivation from our disposition and leave us feeling like victims.

I like saying it this way, "Gratitude is the ultimate re-framer." Once I process my complaints through the lens of gratitude, my perspective changes—immediately.

Just consider all the scientific and proven benefits of gratitude:

◊ More positive feelings

◊ Improved mental health

◊ Improved physical health

◊ Better relationships

◊ Blocks toxic thoughts leading to depression

◊ Strengthens self-esteem

◊ Increases enthusiasm and optimism

Isn't it obvious? When you're grateful, you become exceptional and attract magnificent and exceptional results. A thankful heart is a magnet for miracles.

Once you choose the mindset of gratitude, you're on your way to an extraordinary life. We don't always get to choose what happens from one day to the next, but we get to choose an attitude of gratitude *in* all circumstances. How beautiful you are in this season of life when you choose thankfulness. Midlife will look and feel different, as you are not only grateful for where you've been and what you've experienced, but for where you're going. By faith, thank God, and live in expectation of the remarkable life your grateful heart attracts.

But if gratitude invites miracles, what does ingratitude bring? Ruin.

Ingratitude is the ruin of your soul.

We often talk about the benefits of gratitude, but I also want you to be aware of the consequences of ingratitude; when you don't appreciate all God has blessed you with.

To me, the results of ingratitude are horrifying:

◊ **Negativity.** Without gratitude, only the shadow side of life is seen and embraced.

◊ **Unhappiness.** Tortured by the joy of others, comparisons cause you to focus on what you don't have instead of what you do.

◊ **Entitlement.** Instead of serving the world, you think the world is here to serve you because the world owes you.

◊ **Greed.** An insatiable desire for more and gnawing discontent develops despite the blessings you have.

◊ **Narcissism.** Ingratitude demands your undivided attention. It forever cries out; *What about me?*

◊ **Loneliness.** Ingratitude can lead to the destruction of friendships and meaningful relationships.

◊ **Jealousy.** "It's hard to celebrate others when I fear they will outshine me," says the spirit of an ingrate.

◊ **Critical Spirit.** When ingratitude grips you at your core, you'll soon discover that nothing is ever enough. Nothing brings lasting joy.

The Gratitude Mindset puts an end to the selfish, layered self that fears not being enough. At its roots, ingratitude is the fear of insufficiency—*I'm not enough, I don't have enough.* Nothing is enough.

Today, BraveHeart, you are enough. You have everything you need. You're unlimited in potential and possibility because the source of your life is unlimited. So, thank God in advance for all that you're hoping for. Unleash your grateful heart before you ever hold your dreams in your hand. Your gratitude is a magnet for blessings. Shout Amen.

For the Lord God is brighter than the brilliance of a sunrise! Wrapping himself around me like a shield, he is so generous with his gifts of grace and glory. Those who walk

*along his paths with integrity will never lack one thing
they need, for he provides it all!*

—Psalm 84:11-12 TPT

The Genius Mindset

There's a genius inside of you. You've got problem-solving creativity. You're not a victim. Holding a genius mindset shows you're powerful beyond your wildest dreams. Be free. Shed anything that even resembles a victim mindset.

A victim says,

- ◊ The world is out to get me.
- ◊ I can't do it.
- ◊ It's not my fault.
- ◊ It's because of them, him, her, that I'm like this.
- ◊ No one will help me. I'm all alone.
- ◊ I can never change.
- ◊ Misfortune always happens to me.

The sorrowful refrain of echoes from the lips of the victim, as they lament, "Life is cruel and unjust. Everything bad happens to me," the victim believes by no choice of their own.

But a victorious mindset says, "I can face this hardship. Everything happens for me. I have autonomy and choice. I'm capable of solving problems and overcoming negative circumstances." When you own a victorious mindset, you don't deny your emotions; you feel them but deny their right to control and defeat you.

With a genius mindset, you take 100 percent responsibility for your choices and emotional condition. You alone manage your feelings, decisions, actions, and reactions. No one makes you feel or do anything.

Genius means, "Exceptional intellectual or creative power or other natural ability."

I have chosen to use the word genius because of the second part of that definition: *exceptional creative power.* The God of the universe made us in his image and filled us with the Holy Spirit. We are not victims in this world. Instead, we are empowered, creative overcomers.

Accepting this mindset will transform your life.

The Gritty Mindset

I'll tell you a secret about me. I love the word grit and what it represents. I'm a resilient, down-and-dirty, hang-on kind of gal. I don't quit. I dig in and persevere. I think life has forced me to either cry uncle and throw in the towel, or rise up, brush myself off, and keep going. In keeping with my temperament style, I choose to continue on and endure.

This is grit.

The ability to keep going, believing that, in time, hard work, patience, and endurance will bring great reward. As I think of it, I come from a long line of resilient women, and I'm thankful for that heritage. I'm really tempted to write about how women have been shamed out of their resilience and grit, but I suppose that's another book. But if you come from a line of strong women, don't regret that. Use your heritage as fuel to direct your strength into a positive path for God.

Back to grit …

A gritty mindset is characterized by resilience—the ability to spring back quickly from failed attempts and hardship—and a positive frame for failure itself. As Tony Robbins says, "There is no failure only results." If we view ourselves as failures, or having failed at something, we end up feeling defeated and unmotivated to keep going or try again. If, however, we realize failure is an event not a person, and we recognize failure is the most information rich experience for us, and we can quickly reframe our experience as something positive. Instead of a defeated mindset saying, "I failed," or worse, "I'm a failure," bravehearted women say with confidence, "I learned," or "These results are not as good as I had hoped, so I'll adjust and try again."

How empowering is that? Very.

This gritty mindset will keep you from quitting and accepting the status quo, fortifying you to stay brave and take all the right steps that lead you to reaching your goals.

"Have a fierce resolve in everything you do."

"Demonstrate determination, resiliency, and tenacity."

"Do not let temporary setbacks become permanent excuses."

"Use mistakes and problems as opportunities to get better—not reasons to quit." Angela Duckworth[15]

The Generous Mindset
You can trust in abundance.

The Generous Mindset firmly believes that there is enough *whatever* to go around. Enough talent, wealth, giftedness, opportunity, love, friends, and more. A generous mindset says, "I can give my support to you because I know your success doesn't limit mine." There's unlimited abundance in this life. So, trust what God has determined for you will come to you if you are prepared to receive it.

A generous mindset is an abundance mindset, and possessing one will set you free from jealousy, comparisons, and competitive striving. Listen bravehearted woman, you are running *your* race, not someone else's. God has more than enough blessings to bestow on you. Rejoice with those who rejoice. You are still positioned for greatness and success. In fact, if you sow generously into the successful outcome of someone else, you double your blessings—the ones you have coming because of your inheritance in God and the ones you have planted and invested in for a return. Too many people get stuck because they without the generous release of compliments, appreciation, blessings, financial investment, and support of others for fear that they will be left behind.

Renounce the hoarding and scarcity mindset and step into abundance and generosity.

The Gaining Edge Mindset

Success results from small but significant and positive actions, done repeatedly and consistently. This attitude is the gaining edge mindset. It says baby steps matter, and don't just make *a* difference—they make *all* the difference.

I first learned this principle in 2010 when I read Jeff Olsen's book, *The Slight Edge: Turning Simple Disciplines into Massive Success and Happiness.* Olsen shares the principle that every action we take leads us either closer of further away from our goals. He writes, "Greatness is always in the moment of the decision. And so is fate. The wisdom to recognize the slight edge, shows up in the mundane little choices we make every day. Not in some big dramatic moment with the orchestra swelling in crescendo behind us and those private unseen everyday moments are what determine the path your life will take."

After 13 years of applying the slight edge philosophy, I can tell you it will change your life. It has changed mine.

I've discovered taking baby steps in the right direction is easy to do, and unfortunately taking baby steps in the wrong direction is also easy to do. So, I tell myself often, "some push-ups are better than no push-ups. Some savings are better than no savings. Some dietary restrictions are better than no restrictions." That means I've adopted the Gaining Edge Mindset—my adaptation of the slight edge—philosophy and I live my life by it. I no longer dismiss small actions that seem insignificant, or spout words like, "Go big or go home." Quantum leaps and windfalls of success are rare. If we always wait for the right time, or money, or any other perfect condition before we take positive and beneficial action, we will wait a lifetime. And whether or not you know it, the slight edge is working right now, either for you or against you.

> *The slight edge is relentless; it cuts both ways. Used productively it carries you up towards success. Used carelessly it pulls you towards failure. Simple productive actions, repeated consistently over time. Simple errors in judgement, repeated consistently over time. Your choice is really that simple.*
>
> —Jeff Olsen.

The Genuine Mindset

We've already talked about authenticity and the importance for you to live from your true self. The Genuine Mindset, re-emphasizes that philosophy. In your bravehearted midlife journey, it's time for you to live from your genuine passion and purpose.

You've found your voice and you don't have to say yes to everyone and everything out of obligation, people pleasing, or fear. You can firmly and confidently state your values and opinions, without insecure hesitation. As my daughter, Lisa, told me the other day, "Mom, today I know who I am and I can finally say with boldness, my favorite color is purple."

Good job daughter.

Freedom to be yourself is exactly how an international, million-member organization for midlife women was formed. Sue Ellen Cooper, a commercial artist, founded the organization quite by accident, when she sent a poem entitled, *Warning*, by Jenny Joseph, to her friend who was turning 55. The opening line of the poem reads,

> *When I am an old woman, I shall wear purple with a red hat which doesn't go, and doesn't suit me.*

Sue Ellen included a red hat with the poem as a gift to her friend. Sue Ellen sent the poem and red hat combo to several more girlfriends on their birthdays. One day, Sue Ellen and her friends decided to gather for lunch, all donning their wild red hats and flamboyant purple outfits. That April afternoon in 1998, five ladies in whimsical clothing birthed what is now known as the Red Hat Society. According to their website the society is "A worldwide membership society that encourages women in their quest to get the most out of life. We support women in the pursuit of Fun, Friendship, Freedom, Fitness and the Fulfillment of lifelong dreams."

You may not be ready to be a red-hatter, but don't miss the principle of embracing your authentic, genuine self. You will liberate yourself to live in your passion and purpose, not under obligation or fear.

7 G-Fierce Mindsets

Each of the 7 Mindsets of a bravehearted woman requires awareness, intentionality, and practice as you choose to renew your mind in this way:

◊ Choose a Growth Mindset over a Fixed Mindset

◊ Choose a Grateful Mindset over Ingratitude

◊ Choose a Genuis Mindset over Victimhood

◊ Choose a Gritty Mindset over Failure

◊ Choose a Generous Mindset over Scarcity

◊ Choose a Gaining Edge Mindset over Quantum Leaps

◊ Choose a Genuine Mindset over People Pleasing

If you apply your time and attention to these mindsets you'll begin to readily identify when you've slipped into a negative pattern. Ask yourself, "*How am I thinking right now? Am I in victim mode? Was that thought from a generous, abundant mindset or from scarcity? Am I thinking and acting like failure is a person or can I apply a grit mindset and set myself free?*"

Your mindset is your future, so …

Pause.

Ponder.

Pick.

Your mind is a garden. Your thoughts are the seeds. The harvest can either be flowers or weeds.

—William Wordsworth

The world as we have created it is a process of our thinking. It cannot be changed without changing our thinking.

—Albert Einstein

Brave Challenge #7: Choose

Which of the 7 Mindsets do you need to improve the most?

Decide one step you can take to grow and become better in the mindset you chose.

Fortitude 4: Craft Virtuous Talk.
I Say

What you say can preserve life or destroy it; so you must
accept the consequences of your words.

—Proverbs 18:21

What kinds of words come out of your mouth?"

That question was posed to me one day. I was sure I would ace this area of beautiful, virtuous speech because I tried to speak good, uplifting, and positive words. So, I bravely took the 24-hour challenge presented by the speaker. "For the next 24 hours, listen to your words and your thoughts, and become a learner of you. Discover if your words are life-giving."

After 24 hours of half-hearted observation, the results of my speech challenge mortified me. Critical, judgmental, insecure, self-deprecating words, thoughts, and ideas rolled effortlessly from my mouth--and my heart. Without realizing it, I had let my verbal guard down inch by inch, and I was becoming exactly who I said I was and how I thought about myself. My speech desperately needed a faith-lift.

This may be true for you, too.

What words come out of your mouth? Are they uplifting and life-giving? Or are they words of doubt, discouragement, or death? You have two choices—that's it. You can speak life or death. There are no void or empty words.

As it did me, the 24-hour challenge may show you a need to elevate your speech habits. Do you speak from a place of power, authority, creativity, and positivity? Or would you discover you're ultimately dooming yourself with disempowering and negative words?

In this chapter, my goal is not only to pose the same question to you—what words come out of your mouth—but to persuade you to consider the impact of your words on your life.

Your words have created your present. And your words will create your future.

This is a truth taught by many. Your life results from what you have believed and what you have spoken. If you don't like your present life, listen to the words coming out of your mouth. You'll no doubt discover your tongue is directing the course of your life. You'll be headed for more of the same unless you decide today to change your vocabulary. Instead of using words to curse your circumstances, use your words to create the life you want. Speak life, love, victory, and success.

Words Create Worlds

Many people only speak about "what is." By saying how they feel, what's wrong, what they lack, and what their world is like. This speech is *reporting* and will produce more of the same results. But when we use our words to speak what *should be*, not just *what is*, we create the life we long for.

As Joel Osteen says, "Don't use your words to describe your situation; instead, use your words to change your situation." An example for us to follow is found in the Scripture in Romans Chapter 4. Before a man named Abraham ever had a child, God called him a father and the *Father of Many Nations.* God used words to create and call into existence what is not yet visible. Verse 17 says, "God, who gives life to the dead and calls those things which do not exist as though they did." (NKJV)

We can follow God's example and send forth our words to bring life, build up, create beauty, and powerfully change our world.

Here's another way to think about it.

What if everything you say today will come to pass? How would you speak? How careful would you be to eliminate negativity? And how many words would you use to declare health, wealth, wisdom, and love? Well, your words will retrieve the results you are speaking. It may not be today, but you will live with the consequences of your speech. That's because your words are servants sent forth by your mouth to go fetch what you say. If you speak out of doubt, limiting beliefs, and lack, your words—aka, your servants—will bring that fruit back to you.

Now you may say, "Dawn, this seems far-fetched. In fact, I've tried speaking positively, and it doesn't work for me. I'm still broke, in a job I hate, and discouraged over my weight. My joints hurt, I have no energy, and I can't lose one pound."

It's just negatively working against you. You're getting more of exactly what you're saying.

I can't emphasize it enough—words contain great power. Once spoken and released into the atmosphere, your words go into motion to produce results for you because there's an assignment on each word you speak—bring death, destruction, ruin, defeat, or bring life—strength, growth, increase, encouragement, and joy.

Do your words inspire faith?

Your voice—your words and speech—is the most influential voice in your life. With your words, you can talk yourself into faith (life) or fear (death.) Your vocabulary can pronounce affirmations of goodness and opportunity or declare defeat and destruction. You can persuade yourself to follow the decisions and disciplines you have determined for yourself, or through very convincing rationalizations, you can talk yourself right out of God's will.

Remember, *faith comes by hearing.* (See Romans 10:17) What does your spirit hear you saying?

The language of a bravehearted woman does not express defeat, lack, scarcity, or failure. She does not recite "I-CAN'T-tations." She speaks I-CAN-tations. [16] You are that bravehearted woman, so don't speak doubt and defeat and expect a life of courage and victory. Instead, employ your words to create the kind of life you want to live.

Your words are your future.

Other leaders, coaches, and pastors teach the same truth.

◊   "There is power in words. What you say is what you get." Zig Ziglar

◊   "Words cannot only create emotions; they create actions. And from our actions flow the results of our lives." - Tony Robbins

◊   "Raise your word, not your voice. It is rain that grows flowers, not thunder." - Rumi

◊   "Words are containers for power. You choose what kind of power they carry." - Joyce Meyer

◊   "You can change the course of your life with your words." - Anonymous

◊   "Be careful with your words. Once they are said, they can be only forgiven, not forgotten." - Unknown

Words of the Heart

Your words flow like a river from the core of your innermost being.

God's Word says words are birthed out of the overflow of the heart (core mind and identity)—beautiful words, but also words that defile and pollute us. That means you create the words, and then the words create you. As the late Eugene Peterson, author of "The Message" paraphrase of the Bible, said, "We cannot be too careful about the words we use; we start out using them, and they end up using us." So deeply contemplate the condition of your heart, and tend to it with care. Your heart is the birth place of words, creating your worlds.

As I developed the Five Fortitudes of a BraveHearted Woman, I was keenly aware of how all the fortitudes—vision, identity, mindset, speech, and actions/habits—intricately work together. In the case of words, notice how mindset and words are inseparably linked. It's like a vicious cycle. If you accept the wrong beliefs, you will speak the wrong words. If you speak the wrong words, you will eventually embrace more of the wrong beliefs. If you speak the wrong words and hold the wrong beliefs, you will attract the wrong circumstances. On and on, the cycle continues, creating negative consequences and results.

Consider The Science

Myriads of scientific research show us the powerful impact of our words on our body, mind, and spirit.

In the book, *Words Can Change Your Brain*, Co-Authors Dr. Andrew Newberg, a neuroscientist, and Mark Robert Waldman, a communications expert state,

> *Our brain has given us the potential to communicate in extraordinary ways, and the ways we choose to use our words can improve the neural functioning of the brain. In fact, a single word has the power to influence the expression of genes that regulate physical and emotional stress.*

Furthermore, they state,

> *Exercising positive thoughts can quite literally change one's reality…By holding a positive and optimistic [word] in your mind, you stimulate frontal lobe activity. This area includes specific language centers that connect directly to the motor cortex responsible for moving you into action. And as our research has shown, the longer you concentrate on positive words, the more you begin to affect other areas of the brain.*

Also, Magnetic Resonance Imaging—M.R.I.—evidence suggests certain neural pathways are increased when people speak self-affirmation. The prefrontal cortex becomes more active when we think or talk about our personal values.

Other studies have found that a habit of prolonged negative thinking diminishes your brain's ability to think, reason, and form memories. Pessimism drains your brain's resources.

A recent article on Healthline.com said this:

◊ Negative thinking can increase your risk for developing dementia.

◊ Participants who exhibited repetitive negative thinking had more cognitive decline and problems with memory.

◊ They also had higher levels of tau protein and amyloid deposits, both of which are linked to Alzheimer's disease.

◊ Experts say mindfulness and other techniques can help reduce negative thinking patterns.

Accentuating the positive, eliminating the negative, and latching on to the affirmative may not just put you in a better mood. It's also good for your brain.

I could continue on for chapters. The science is in and proves with all certainty your words shape your reality.

Virtuous Talk

What types of virtuous speech are we talking about? Well, to help kick start your journey to a bravehearted life, consider a solid commitment to these seven standards when speaking:

◊ Speak Words of Life

Our words build up or tear down, encourage or dis-courage, increase faith or ignite doubt, inspire dreams, or kill all hope.

Life or death. That's the power of the tongue. So, the over-arching principle is this: use life-giving, positive speech whenever you communicate. If you don't want the words you speak to come to pass, then don't release them. I've been applying this truth for many years now. If I hear anyone speaking death over themselves, it feels like fingernails on a chalkboard—it makes me cringe. Use your words and influence to birth life. Arrest words of doubt and death and put a gag order on them. If you find yourself in a battle over your words, inspect your heart to see where the pain, hurt, unforgiveness, or bitterness are hiding. Your woundedness is churning out an outward stream of words to describe an inward condition, so pay attention.

Today, choose to speak life-giving words over your:

> ◊ Relationships
>
> ◊ Children
>
> ◊ Spouse

◊ Body

◊ Health

◊ Church

◊ Business

◊ Mind

◊ Future

◊ Finances

◊ Possessions

◊ State Possibilities

As we have noted, speaking about negative circumstances doesn't change or empower you. Rather than using your words to describe what you don't want, recite what is possible. Take a faith stance and state what you believe God will do. Genuinely believe that with God, anything is possible because it is. Find scriptures that strengthen your faith and paste them in highly visible places. Use your journal to write uplifting quotes and Bible verses and read them *to* yourself and *over* yourself daily.

Here are some of my favorites:

◊ "Jesus said, with men this is impossible, but with God all things are possible." —Matthew 19:26

◊ "Nothing is impossible; the word itself says 'I'm possible'." —Audrey Hepburn.

◊ "Behold, I am Yahweh, the God of all flesh. Is there anything too hard for me?" —Jeremiah 32:27

◊ "You become what you believe. And to believe that you are created by the power [God] that's greater than yourself means anything is possible." —Oprah

◊ "For nothing spoken by God is impossible."
—Luke 1:37

◊ "I can do all things through Christ, who strengthens me." —Philippians 4:13

◊ "There is nothing impossible to him who will try."
—Alexander The Great.

◊ "… certainly, I tell you, if you have faith as a grain of mustard seed, you will tell this mountain, move from here to there, and it will move; and nothing will be impossible for you." —Jesus (See Matthew 17:20)

◊ Share Encouragement

Beautiful speech can be found in the mouth of a bravehearted woman when she is generous with her words of blessing and encouragement. I believe our world is starving for words of deep and spiritual affirmation. Speaking beautifully is not to be confused with flattery or insincere praise spoken to further our interest or personal gain. When you feel prompted to offer encouragement to someone, you're most likely being chosen by the Holy Spirit to minister to a person in need. Trust that the message you speak is the "gift of encouragement." See Romans 12:8. Be brave and generous in those moments. Don't hold back. You're being called to "speak life."

"Like apples of gold in settings of silver Is a word spoken at the right time."

—Proverbs 25:11 AMP

◊ Sculpt I-CAN-tations

Two words should never be in the vocabulary of a bravehearted woman … "I can't." Remember, anything's possible. You're more capable than you know.

Instead, employ the word "yet." Your brain knows the difference—and it's a significant difference—between saying

"I *can't* do that,"

and

"I can't do that *yet.*"

One phrase ends with an emphatic period, while the other ends with a comma. A period says it's over, done, final, finito, but a comma leaves room for what is next. By using this simple word, you position yourself to continue growing, reaching, and succeeding in any area you choose. Don't limit God, and don't limit yourself. Learn to push yourself. You'll be amazed.

◊ Secure Positive Labels

Like content labels on a jar, descriptors stick to our minds, persuading us to believe they accurately define what we're "made of." When we accept the man-made label, we surrender our identity and self-worth. Remember, labels don't have to be true to hurt us; we only have to accept them as truth. Eventually, we live into those negative beliefs and attitudes as our inside essence adapts to reflect the outside label.

I challenge you to stop using negative labels over yourself. Those descriptors only lock you into a behavior, habit, or identity you don't want. When you decide, however, on a God-honoring identity that you wish to cultivate and grow into, you can claim a positive label for yourself and develop that character and quality.

As a bravehearted woman, you're ready to shed anything that does not attract your best life or bring you to your destiny. Shed those false identities and reject old descriptions that limit you!

◊ Soothe with Self-Compassion

How often are we tempted to judge ourselves harshly and withhold self-compassion? Many times a day for some of us. We easily and quickly shame ourselves for our shortcomings and idiosyncrasies, criticizing ourselves for not being enough. But rising up brave means we embrace who we are without judging, scolding, criticizing, blaming, or shaming ourselves, either in thought or with our words. Virtuous talk eliminates the verbal lashings we readily dole out on ourselves and replaces the shaming tones with words of compassion, comfort, and truth spoken in love. Not that we get a *pass* to become lazy or soft on ourselves. No. In midlife, we must push ourselves more diligently than ever. Giving up on beneficial disciplines is too easy at this point. Hey, we are women of grit. We do not—will not—quit.

Soothing with compassion means we'll be kind to ourselves and offer ourselves patience and understanding. If you long to fulfill your full potential, you must accept self-compassion. Without it, you won't take risks, try new ideas or push yourself into uncomfortable places. The fear of shame will stop you, and failure will never become your friend.

Several years ago, I stumbled on a proven psychological practice, speaking comforting words to yourself while looking at yourself in the mirror. One of my clients—I'll call her Melissa—struggled with all desperation to overcome her self-rejection and harsh inner critic. She berated herself for everything—her looks, personality, body, and career. On and on went the list. One day, I told her, "Melissa, I want you to go home, look in the mirror and tell yourself, *I love you.* Then I want you to sing *You are so Beautiful,* to yourself." She did as I suggested, and that day was the beginning of her healing. She established a new, kinder relationship with herself and learned to silence her inner bully. Melissa also established a new relationship with her mirror. No longer was the mirror the place where she judged and ridiculed herself. Melissa made it a place of celebration and an opportunity to display kindness to herself.

Here's the challenge for you, too—to love and embrace *you* today. Get in front of that mirror, give yourself a huge high five and the best smile you can possibly muster, and say, *I love you. You're doing a great job, girl.*

Now sing, *You are so Beautiful,* because you are. Today, you're free from uttering words of shame and judgment.

◊ **Slow Down on Apologies**

For way too long now, I've heard women over-apologizing. We may not apologize with our words alone; we do it with our body language—our facial expressions, vocal tones, body posture, and eye contact—all screaming, "I'm sorry!"

I'll confess, I was guilty. For many years, I worked as the only woman in ministry, serving in what was traditionally considered a male-only approved role. On many days, I felt intimidated and out of place. Those feelings of inadequacy stirred in me the need to apologize. I'd enter the boardroom with the other leaders—ten men sitting at the board table—and what do you think happened to me? My shoulders slumped with my head bent low, my eyes darted to my chair, and my voice transformed into some form of a family member from Micky and Minnie.

I became a mouse.

Why? Because of my lack of confidence, I fell prey to the pressure of apologizing to others for "showing up and breathing their air." I'm happy to report I overcame my fear and insecurities and have had a flourishing career, and garnered the respect of my colleagues. Truthfully, with God's help, I was promoted through the ranks and held the top executive role, placing me as the leader over all the men. Yep, I was the Lady Boss.

I hear women over-apologizing because I've been there.

Women apologize when they have differing opinions, speak up in a meeting, walk into a room, or anytime insecurity rears its ugly head.

Have you done that?

Well, as a bravehearted woman, it's time for you to amp up your confidence and ditch those ridiculous apologies.

When apologies are warranted, offer a sincere "I apologize" is the right words to speak. You'll show you have a tender heart and compassionate conscious, and it'll help keep relationships intact. But BraveHeart, if you're over-apologizing and muttering an excessive amount of "I'm sorry," you most likely have a pesky habit that doesn't serve you well.

When you're infected with the "I'm Sorry Habit," you reveal to the world around you:

◊ You have a nervous habit. No one knows why you're apologizing—not even you.

◊ You're insecure and unsure of yourself. You feel the need to make excuses.

◊ You're not willing to stand for what you believe. You apologize even when you're not wrong.

◊ You're ashamed for having needs. You apologize for any deficit.

◊ You're low-self-esteem won't allow people to serve you. You apologize for "putting people out."

◊ You're afraid of rejection. You apologize for asserting yourself.

In the words of Rachel Hollis, Girl, stop apologizing.

Because the world needs your spark. The world needs your energy. The world needs you to show up for your life and take hold of your potential! We need your ideas. We need your love and care. We need your passion. We need your business models. We need to celebrate your successes. We need to watch you rise back up after your failures. We need to see your courage. We need to hear your what if. We need you to stop apologizing for being who you are and become who you were meant to be.

—Rachel Hollis [17]

As I close this chapter, I want to leave you with one more tool I am convinced will shift you out of doubt and defeat into a place of faith and overcoming victory.

Affirmations

Affirmations are simple, concise, and powerful expressions. When you speak, think, and listen to affirmations, these positive statements become thoughts that, in turn, create reality.

Research shows we think about 45,000 to 51,000 different thoughts in a day. That's 150 to 300 thoughts per minute. Sadly, for most people, 80% of these thoughts are negative. Fortunately, affirmations provide a way to speak life over everything that concerns us—our mind, body, soul, finances, relationships, outcomes—everything.

It's simple to practice positive affirmations, but not always easy. Your brain will want to fight with you at first. That's the resistance—cognitive dissonance—you'll feel when truth confronts lies, limiting beliefs, labels, and any fears present. Keep reciting these powerful affirmations; they are re-wiring your brain.

You benefit from using positive affirmations because you

◊   remember your true identity in Christ, and build healthy self-worth and value.

◊   give yourself the courage to make positive changes in your life.

◊   encourage yourself and stoke your spirit to believe God for the desires of your heart.

◊   motivate yourself to act and move on your goals, which boosts motivation to continue those positive actions.

◊   concentrate on your goals as you speak positively.

◊   change your negative thought patterns into positive ones.

◊ influence your subconscious mind to access new beliefs.

◊ feel positive about yourself and boost your self-confidence.

And never let ugly or hateful words come from your mouth, but instead let your words become beautiful gifts that encourage others; do this by speaking words of grace to help them

—Ephesians 4:29-32 TPT

For a list of BraveHearted Affirmations, visit
https://www.braveheartedwoman.com/brave-affirmations

Brave Challenge #8: Listen

For the next 24 hours, listen to your words and your thoughts. Become a learner of you. Determine if your words are uplifting and life-giving. Purge your tongue of harmful words.

Fortitude 5: Commit to Excellent Actions.
I Do

Everything you want is out there waiting for you to ask.
Everything you want also wants you. But you have to take
action to get it.

—Jules Renard

The fifth and final fortitude of a Bravehearted Woman is where all the magic happens. You can have the best dreams, goals, mindsets, and words, but without accompanying actions, you will only ever see your dreams in your head. You must take action.

Faith by itself, if it is not accompanied by action, is dead.

—James 2:17 NIV

If you want to turn your dreams into reality, you'll have to adopt consistent and habitual daily actions that move you closer and closer to achieving your dream.

This is the same advice I gave Rebecca.

Rebecca became a client after listening to my podcast, "The BraveHearted Woman." She shared how inspired she felt after hearing the episode on "Vision: The Secret to Overcoming Discouragement." (Dawn Damon, 2023) At 56, Rebecca had lost hope. Plagued by regret, she felt trapped; trapped in a dull and loathsome full-time job, in a body she didn't want, and stuck in an unfulfilling relationship, Rebecca longed for more, but saw no hope of her life ever changing.

Together, Rebecca and I spent several hours talking, dreaming, and praying about her life.

For Dawn's Podcast, "The BraveHearted Woman" visit

https://dawndamon.com/podcast/

or

https://www.youtube.com/@dawn_damon

Through the "Discovery Process" I've developed, Rebecca connected with her true self and could clearly articulate what she truly desired in life.

We captured all Rebecca wanted to accomplish, goals she wanted to reach—including health, finance, and relational goals—and the changes she longed to make in her life. We developed a detailed plan that, if she followed, would no doubt lead her to fulfillment and success. She left feeling confident and committed to the process.

A few weeks later, Rebecca arrived for her appointment. I was eager to hear the great report she would bring and planned how we would celebrate her progress.

"So, tell me the good news. How are you doing on the action steps of your plan?"

"Well, I haven't started yet. I don't know, I just feel distracted. I'm super busy at work, which is hard because I hate my job. I can't wait to get out of it. I have almost no time and well, to be honest, I'm doubting."

"Ah, tell me more about that doubt, Rebecca. What specifically has you wavering?"

"Everything, she admitted. I doubt myself. I doubt my ability. I doubt my dream is viable. I doubt I'm brave enough to take the leap."

"I think I understand what's going on here. Insecurity has you doubting in the darkness what God gave you in the light. If we were to take the mask off of your doubt, we'd see it's actually fear. You are in a battle. Fear wants to disrupt your commitment to growth and stop you from implementing your plan. But your inaction is creating more doubt for you. You must face fear with planned action. You have a great plan, Rebecca. All you have to do is take one small baby step at a time."

Dale Carnegie says, "Inaction breeds doubt and fear. Action breeds confidence and courage. If you want to conquer fear, do not sit home and think about it. Go out and get busy."

Rebecca needed to get busy, to take actions that would ignite her confidence.

I wish I could tell you that Rebecca broke free of fear that day, applied the Five Fortitudes, and soared into a new destiny. But it didn't happen. Not that way. She slipped back into her misery for another year—feeling like a failure and remaining stuck. But God is faithful. He had more in store for Rebecca and he was going to complete the good work he had started, just as he promises. "I am convinced and confident of this very thing, that He who has begun a good work in you will [continue to] perfect and complete it" (Philippians 1:6 AMP).

Rebecca got back on track and began acting. Inch by inch she implemented the steps we strategically planned. Her enthusiasm for life elevated and her self-esteem rose. As I write this chapter, I'm watching the miracle of Rebecca unfold. She is transforming before my very eyes.

What happened?

She solidified her commitment for transformation and took action! With a firm commitment to get moving, Rebecca dusted off her strategic plan, re-gained clarity around her dreams and goals, and with all the confidence she could muster, took the next right baby step.

Until one is committed there is hesitancy, the chance to draw back, always ineffectiveness. Concerning all acts of initiative or creation, there is one elementary truth... that the moment one definitely commits oneself, then Providence moves. too. All sorts of things occur to help one that would otherwise never have occurred. A whole stream of events issues from the decision, raising in ones' favor all manner of incidents and meetings and material assistance which no man would have believed would have come his way. Whatever you think you can do or believe you can do, begin it. Action has magic, grace, and power in it.

—W.H. Murray

Are You Ready?

Don't worry if you're not clear on the actions you should take to reach your goals just yet. The right, brave steps of action are not always obvious and creating a plan of action takes thought, energy, and time. In the next chapter we will investigate what specific actions you should incorporate in your life to achieve all that you dream of!

But first, in this chapter, I'm going to show you how to create and deploy the kind of habits that will catapult your life into the next level; the level of success and fulfillment. In fact, you'll become unstoppable.

You simply can't stay stuck in mediocre when you combine clarity—the *what* to do—with excellent habits and strategic action, the how to do it. Mix in the other four fortitudes you've learned and you'll be making so much progress toward your goals and dreams that others will sit up and take note of you saying, "Wow. What's going on with you?"

My question to you is, are you ready?

Do you believe there is more for you? Don't let another year pass you by before you take action that leads to the transformation you desire. No need to wander through this life aimless for one more moment. You *can* dream again. You can change and find clarity and reach goals you never thought possible. That's what being a bravehearted woman is all about. I'm inviting you into the life God has for you.

God has a "Yes" in-store for you.

Are *you* ready to say yes?

Action is a great restorer and builder of confidence.
Inaction is not only the result, but the cause, of fear.
Perhaps the action you take will be successful; perhaps
different action or adjustments will have to follow. But
any action is better than no action at all.

—Norman Vincent Peale

A Look at Habits

Personal growth and becoming a bravehearted woman, building first-rate, gold-medal habits is the most important skill you can cultivate.

Good habits bring joy, blessing, abundance, success, and more. Bad habits lead to defeat, disappointment, debt, and guilt.

You're here to live an outstanding life and be a positive influence in the world. But you won't have life par excellence with poor, pathetic habits.

So first, become a student of your habits. I know … Here we go again with self-discovery and awareness. But God's Word says, "my people are destroyed from lack of knowledge" (Hosea 4:6 NIV). Ignorance may be bliss for a moment, but in the end, a lack of knowledge will destroy you. I don't want you to be unaware of how your unconscious habits may be at the root of your inability to overcome problems and succeed in life. We'll talk more about mindfulness and self-awareness later in this chapter.

John Maxwell teaches, "the secret to your success is found in your daily routine."

The actions you take *or don't take* every day are bringing you somewhere. Whether good or bad, your habits produce clear and obvious results. What you do in private will be revealed and rewarded in public. What reward do you think your habits will bring you? What will they reveal about you? We may look at successful, high-achieving people and say to ourselves, *That's what I want to have someday.* But the real issue is not do you want what they have, but do you want to do what they did to have what they have? We see the public *reward* of their life, but we don't see the private, hidden moments of blood, sweat, and tears.

Habits Defined

James Clear, author of *Atomic Habits* says, "Habits are the small decisions you make and actions you perform every day." Author of *The Power of Habit*, Charles Duhigg says, "Habits are the choices that all of us deliberately make at some point, and then stop thinking about but continue doing, often every day." Ph.D. Stuart Walesh says, "Habits are involuntary behaviors controlled by the subconscious mind."

Putting it all together we discover.

1. Habits are consistent.
2. Habits are both consciously and unconsciously performed.
3. Habits are chosen and learned behaviors.

Now listen to this staggering research on habits: Studies by neurobiologists, cognitive psychologist, and others tell us that anywhere from 40 to 90 percent of human behavior is done through habit. That means that most of what we do, what we say, how we think, and how we feel is automatic, habitual, and sometimes undetected.

When I learned of that statistic, I became curious. *How many actions do I perform in a day that are controlled by my unconscious?* I came up with a list of the many ways my habits were shaping my life. Tony Robbins says, "Every action you take is fuel for the kind of person you want to be or become. Success is the product of many right choices … that become daily habits. In essence, if we want to direct our lives, we must take control of our consistent actions. It's not what we do once in a while that shapes our lives, but what we do consistently."

So, take a look at this expanded list of habits and use it as a gauge to ask yourself the same question.

What habits do I have in these areas and how are they shaping my life?

What are my ...

Physical and Health Habits

◊   Sleep

◊   Eat

◊   Exercise

◊   Sexual

Relational Habits

◊   Attachment style

◊   Choosing a mate or friend

- ◊ Communication style

- ◊ Managing conflict

- ◊ Roles –victim or hero

Financial Habits

- ◊ Spending

- ◊ Saving

- ◊ Investing

- ◊ Giving

- ◊ Hoarding

- ◊ Risk adverse or tolerant

Self-Defeating Habits

- ◊ Excuse making

- ◊ Rationalizing

- ◊ Procrastination

- ◊ Quitting

- ◊ Feeling rejected and withdrawing

- ◊ Fearing

- ◊ Reacting

Mindset and Thinking Habits

- ◊ Inflexible

- ◊ Fixed mindset

◊ Spontaneous

◊ Impetuous

◊ Negative, problem-identifying

◊ Judging

◊ Shaming

◊ Anxiety, worry, panic

◊ Victim

Speaking and Listening Habits

◊ Naysaying

◊ Interrupting

◊ One-Upping

◊ Defensive

◊ Encouraging

◊ Blaming

◊ Silence

◊ Stonewalling

◊ Criticizing

Social Habits

◊ Eating

◊ Drinking

◊ People interaction

◊ Withdrawal and isolation

  ◊   Self-protective

  ◊   Bragging

  ◊   Presenting the false self, wearing masks

Coping Habits

  ◊   Emotional filters

  ◊   Responding in anger

  ◊   Intimidation

  ◊   Humor

  ◊   Retaliation

  ◊   Name-calling

  ◊   Fight or flight

Spiritual Habits

  ◊   Prayer

  ◊   Meditation

  ◊   Communion with God

  ◊   Bible reading

  ◊   Worshipping

Development and Growth Habits

  ◊   Reading

  ◊   Training

  ◊   Experiencing

◊ Resilience

◊ Curiosity

Our life is the sum of our habits. Craig Groeschel said on a recent episode of his podcast, *The Leadership Podcast*, "When you're born you look like your parents. When you die, you look like your habits!"

As a bravehearted woman, you must know the nature of your habits.

What habits serve you well? Are they working for you and "putting you on the path toward success," as James Clear says? Name them and become intentional about continuing the good habits.

What habits do not work well for you, but in fact, work against you, hold you down, and cause you to relapse into defeat? Name those habits too. Be tenacious about changing any harmful habits.

No matter how small and insignificant your good or bad habits may seem to you, they have a trajectory and an accumulating effect.

Consider the long-term consequences of your habits.

If you don't make an adjustment to your habit, where will it lead you? Not simply after doing the habit once or twice, but long-term. If you keep doing this action, where will it lead you in one, three, or five years? If you want to predict where you'll end up in life, all you have to do is follow the curve of the tiny gains or tiny losses that your daily rituals produce to see if you'll arrive in the winner's circle.

Brian Tracey puts it this way, "In five years you will arrive." The question is *where* will you arrive? The answer is, you will arrive exactly where your habits lead you. Good or bad.

I think you get the point, but let me reiterate the idea.

If you eat a bowl of ice cream one night for a bedtime snack, it will have little impact on your health and weight goals. If you eat ice cream every night as your nighttime routine, where do you think you'll be in one year? Well, the Cleveland Clinic says a pint of ice cream every day contains between 150-360 calories, with a probable weight gain of 15 to

36 pounds within a year. That ice cream habit, over time, is shaping you. Literally.

If, however, you have a morning routine of drinking a glass of water with lemon, overtime where do you think that habit will lead you? You'll reap the numerous benefits of hydration—better kidney function, weight loss, flexible joints, better brain function, reversed aging, and so much more. You'll even crave more water as your body's desire for drinking water will increase. This water-drinking habit is creating a healthy mind and body for you, and is a habit you'll want to continue.

The bottom line? We humans are creatures of habits- so make your habits work for you.

Habits Create Results

Success is the accumulative result of consistent daily habits. It's not just one moment of fortune that leads you to your destiny, but your success is the product of intentionality. You've designed a great life. We don't wake up to find we've accidentally fallen into average. No, we've arrived at a dreary funk-filled life by the accumulation of detrimental habits, dreamless, lack luster actions, and a boring daily existence.

Ouch, that's a hard reality.

But painfully true.

Your life is the product of compounding habits.

Your outcomes are a lagging measure of your habits. Your net worth is a lagging measure of your financial habits. Your weight is a lagging measure of your eating habits. Your knowledge is a lagging measure of your learning habits. Your clutter is a lagging measure of your cleaning habits. You get what you repeat.

—James Clear

Don't miss this important point here, your future will be the product of future habits. You can change the trajectory of your life today by making small adjustments. Tiny tweaks turn into enormous rewards.

It's never too late to be who you might have been.

—George Elliot

They Say Breaking Up Is Hard to Do

Perhaps by now you've identified some habits that need to be modified or stopped altogether. If you've got iron-clad discipline, you may end the habit cold-turkey. For most of us, however, changing our behavior will require a process. Either way, the good news is, you can break-up with your bad habits and begin new ones. You've learned those behaviors and guess what? You can also unlearn them.

The time it takes to break a habit depends on several factors, according to research.

Variables include:

◊ how long you've had the habit. How deeply grooved the neuro pathway has become.

◊ the emotional, physical, or social needs the habit fulfills.

◊ whether you have support or help to break the habit.

◊ the physical or emotional reward the habit provides.

The best way to break-up with a negative habit is to first understand that habits have a structure. Turns out, every habit—good or bad—starts

141

with a pattern that neuropsychologists call a "habit-loop." This habit-loop is a process which includes three parts: the cue, the behavior, and the reward.

◊   The Cue is the trigger that starts the habit loop. Something reminds or *cues* the brain to allow the behavior to unfold. Thus, the behavior is prompted and the routine begins.

◊   The Behavior is the actual habit or routine itself.

◊   The Reward is something the brain likes and feels pleasure during or after the routine. This reward informs the brain to activate the habit-loop again in the future.

Once you've identified the habit you want to break, the following steps have proven helpful to end habits.

Mindful Observation

Cues and triggers initiate the habit-loop. Use mindfulness and your powers of observation to explore what prompted your impulse to act. Was it hunger, time of day, a familiar place, boredom, isolation, or an emotion you don't want to feel? Try to develop an awareness of what's going on around and inside you, without judging or shaming yourself. When you understand what's cuing your brain to crave this habit, you're better empowered to catch the prompts, interrupt the pattern, change your physiology, and alter the routine. If you want to break the habit even faster, make the bad habit behavior impossible to do.

Next, become aware and pay attention to what you're gaining as a reward. How is this behavior gratifying you? This step isn't always easy to figure out. Many times, the reward feeds an unconscious need. However, if you stay mindful of your habit-loop long enough, you'll find clues to how this behavior is *temporarily* rewarding you. Remind yourself of the greater reward—achieving your goals and dreams.

For example, Sarah wants to explore her pesky habit of snacking late at night. She decides to apply mindfulness to understand what prompts her cravings and behavior.

One evening, as she's about to reach for a bag of chips, she interrupts herself, takes a deep breath and pauses. *Why am I doing this? Am I really hungry?* Sarah's answer to her own question brings some revelation.

First, she realizes the cue. She's sitting on her couch, a familiar spot for crunching Cheetos. Next, she becomes aware of the trigger… the time. It's around 8:00 PM when feelings of restless and stress about the tasks for the next day tend to roll in.

By applying mindfulness, Sarah discovers that the craving to snack arises from a combination of factors. She feels a mild rumbling in her tummy, but her habit isn't really about genuine hunger. Instead, it's more about satisfying a desire to distract herself from thoughts and feelings of anxiety, which is the reward she derives from the behavior. Sarah admits she's turning to snacks for comfort.

Now, by understanding the cues and triggers that initiate her habit loop, Sarah is empowered to disrupt the pattern. Instead of pouncing on the chips at the cue-triggering hour, she decides to forego the mindless munching, and practice deep breathing with a brief meditation to address her anxiety. This new routine helps her respond to emotions in a more constructive way, ultimately leading to the alteration of her routine and the potential elimination of her late-night snacking habit.

Strategic Replacement

It's not enough to break a habit or stop negative behaviors. You must replace the old, unwanted habit with a new, more empowering, strategic behavior. Say you want to stop drinking a sugary coke every afternoon when you feel an energy slump. If you simply try to avoid the coke machine, you'll likely fall back into the habit when a moment of dire thirst arrives. But if you replace the coke with a healthy option of sparkling water, you strategically replace the old habit with a new, more desirable habit that leads to the outcomes you want. As you repeat the new behavior, the impulse to follow the new routine develops. That's because new habits are formed by repetition, not just days on a calendar. Eventually, once you repeat this new behavior over and over again, you'll start seeing a positive reward from the new habit—more energy, less sugar, more weight loss—the urge to keep this positive behavior will outweigh the desire to repeat the old.

Purposeful Why

Why do you want to change this habit? How is it hurting you now or how will it hurt you if you continue this behavior? Remember *why* you want to change this habit. Remember what this behavior-trap is costing you and how it's holding you back. One positive way to stay connected to your *why* is to use stickers, sticky notes, vision boards, even write it on your hand. Use any visual reminder to post in all the places where you may be tempted to fall back into your habit. Then, wherever the habit-loop—cue, behavior, reward—is triggered, your notes will help you rethink the action.

Motivating Praise

Breaking a deep-rooted habit is difficult. Sometimes incredibly difficult. So, congratulate yourself for any baby steps you've taken and the progress you've made toward transformation. Get in front of that mirror (*you know how much we like mirrors*) and give yourself a high-five, atta baby, and pat on the back. Whatever motivates and cheers you on. When you focus on how far you've come and the courage it took to start a new pattern, you're less likely to discouraged yourself with negative self-talk.

Trusted Support

Finally, ask a trusted friend to support you. Your desire to break poor habits and install new ones will succeed quicker when you add an element of accountability and encouragement. A confidant can offer you the extra motivation you need when you feel tired and alone.

There is great hope, my BraveHeart. You're not bound to behaviors that sabotage your forward progress. Studies show that it's never too late to stop or start new habits and learn new actions. Your brain is malleable throughout your life, and you can change. At long last the myth is dispelled—you *can* teach an old dog new tricks! *Wink.*

Baby Steps Toward Good Habits and Actions

Small, seldom-seen habits have the power to bear us irresistibly toward our destiny.

—Philosopher and Psychologist William James.

Don't you wish you could just download an application called "Good Habits?" I know I've fantasized about finding the easy button that would bring me instant improvement with just one push.

But … *another spoiler alert…* there is no app we can download, no express lane, no easy button, or shortcut to take in creating powerful habits and actions that will lead us to a life we love. No, we must intentionally pursue our goals with diligent work and steps of courageous action.

There is no elevator to success, you have to take the stairs.

—Zig Ziglar

You don't have to start with great energy and gusto to begin a new habit and routine. If you wait to have feelings of motivation or enthusiasm to implement new behaviors, you might not ever get going. Don't wait to feel excited or fearless before you take action.

Forget inspiration. Habit is more dependable. Habit will sustain you whether you're inspired or not.

—Octavia Butler

Motivation follows action, or as I like to say, "inspiration follows perspiration." Just take a baby step. One of my favorite Proverbs says, "Steady plodding brings prosperity ..." (Proverbs 21:5a NLT). This verse reinforces the principle that small, consistent actions will lead you to success.

When you start a new habit, tell yourself you only have to do this new behavior for 10 minutes and then you can stop. Just start. Once you move forward in personal growth and improvement, your inspiration will flow. You'll be so happy you're taking control of your life; a new sense of empowerment and drive will rise within you.

Progress. Just make progress. It's okay to have setbacks and the need for do-overs. It's okay to draw a line in the sand and start over again - and again. Just make sure you're moving the line forward. Move forward. Take baby steps... Then change will come. And it will be good.

—Lysa TerKeurst

How to Successfully Start a New Habit

The women I coach sometimes ask, "How long will it take for me to make this new habit? Three weeks?" They really want to know how long before this new discipline becomes easy and I won't have to think about doing it.

Well, we have traditionally taught it takes 21 days to create a new habit and 90 days to integrate the habit as part of your lifestyle. But as James Clear points out,

*There are all sorts of myths about how long it takes to build
a new habit: 21 days, 30 days, 66 days. The truth is there
is nothing about time passing that magically forms of habit.
Habits are created, based on repetition and frequency, not
by the clock ticking. The next 30 days can pass and you can
do something once or you can do it 100 times.*

—James Clear

Choose a habit that aligns with your vision and goals.

Determination and discipline become easier when you know the habit you want to create leads you toward achieving your goals. Ask yourself, does this behavior align with my values? My dreams? My future vision of where I want to go? If you answer yes, you've found a habit that is congruent with who you are and where you want to go. Resistance will give way when you're convinced this habit is taking you to your destiny.

Choose one habit and start small.

Choose one habit to focus on so you can easily integrate the new behavior into your daily routine. If your goal is to start a new habit of exercise, start with 10 minutes a day and gradually increase your duration. Starting small and having success increases the likelihood that you'll continue on with your new routine. If you're implementing too many new habits or you've set your ambition too high, you may fail, feel discouraged, and quit.

Instead, start small, stay consistent and repetitive.

Choose an anchor.

Anchoring is an effective strategy to start a new habit and involves linking (anchoring) your new habit to an existing habit. For example, when I decided I wanted to do 15 squats a day, I linked that desired behavior with brushing my teeth. Since my dental hygiene was a firmly established routine—consistent action, time, and place—I added an action to that existing ritual. I learned to grab my toothbrush and start squatting. What was I doing? Establishing a cue-based routine for my new habit by linking it to another consistent habit. Instead of just saying, "I want to do 15 squats a day," I decided what, when, and where.

What I would do—15 squats

When I would do it—when I brush my teeth

Where I would do it—the bathroom.

Now the cue is automatic. My brain has anchored the two habits together. As the truism states, "Neurons that fire together wire together." Today, when I brush, I squat.

Choose a reward.

One reason habits stick with us is because of the reward we receive from them.

For example, many of us drink coffee in the morning. We could practically make that delicious brew in our sleep because we know the routine so well. It's our habit and like all habits, it begins with the cue.

The Cue: the morning alarm goes off and so does the trigger for coffee.

The Routine: we make our way to the kitchen, grind the beans, pour in the water, and wait.

The Reward: the hot coffee touches our lips and swirls down our throat.

Connect your new habit with a powerful reward at the end of successfully performing the routine. If you want to exercise in the morning, maybe you hold off on that coffee until your 20-30 minutes of sweating to the oldies is done. Or listen to a favorite audible book only when you're exercising. You can choose anything small or big for the reward. Just make sure it is something you actually *crave,* and you consistently reward yourself with it after executing the new habit.

Take Action

What habits do you want to rid yourself of to make room for new, more empowering habits?

What steps of courage do you want to start or continue?

In the next chapter, I'll outline the 7 Habits successful people practice in their daily lives. Habits that you, as a bravehearted woman, will also want to install so you can live the amazing life God has designed for you.

Are you in earnest? Seize this very minute—What you can do, or dream you can, begin it, Boldness has genius, power, and magic in it, only engage, and then the mind grows heated—Begin it, and the work will be completed!

—Johann Wolfgang von Goethe

Brave Challenge #9: Action

Write this phrase on a sticky note and post it on your mirror:

It's not what I do occasionally that makes me fail or succeed. It's what I do every day that adds up, creating an average or extraordinary life. I choose extraordinary.

Part 3: The BraveHearted Woman

Chapter Eleven

Habits of a BraveHearted Woman

One day, she discovered that she was fierce and strong and
full of fire and that not even she could hold herself back
because her passion burned brighter than her fears.

—Mark Anthony

I pray by now, BraveHeart, after reading about the 5-Fortitudes, you've discovered a fresh fire.

I pray you've become hungry and a fierce craving for your best life has awakened within you. And with this awakening, I hope you'll rise and feed this hunger.

Don't be satisfied with meager portions of God's abundance when the table of opportunity is lavishly set before you. May your vision be clear and burn brighter than your fears.

Believe in yourself.

God does.

So do I.

Take heart, be brave, and stand with confidence. God is making you into a strong, wise, and courageous woman. You've got what it takes to live wholeheartedly. You're not afraid of hard work. You make no excuses; you're ready to win.

Yes, you!

If my words inspire you and you're ready for the next challenge, let's explore together what the 7 Habits of a successful, fulfilled, and brave woman look like. These are the habits that practically all successful people on the planet practice. And by success, I mean those living with vision and purpose, achieving goals, and stewarding their body, relationships, and finances well. Success to me is experiencing God's wholeness, health, and ultimate purpose for your body, soul, and spirit.

I've practiced the habits I will share with you for more than a decade now, and I can tell you they have changed my life. After my unwanted divorce, the word *unwanted*, described the next year of my life.

I felt unnecessary and unloved. The rejection I experienced was brutal. I often said I felt as if I was thrown out on the curb like unpleasant trash. My confidence was decimated.

My circumstances were desolate. Nothing about my life looked familiar. I thought I had lost everything. And in reality, my losses were immense. I lost my spouse, my family unit, my job, my church, eventually, my house. I told God many times, "This testimony is unwanted."

My future seemed vacant. How could I go on? What would I do? How would I make a living?

I knew I had to pull myself together. I couldn't change what happened to me, but I could change me. I controlled my choices, how I felt about my life, and how I would think and behave. Surely, God saw this plot twist coming into my story. He has a plan for my good and a future hope for me. I reminded myself often. See Jeremiah 29:11.

It was time to turn my unwanted life into one I desired and loved. I had to rid myself of my faint heart, change my mindset, and become brave. So, I slowly implemented the habits I will share with you, gradually adding each one until I consistently and automatically practiced all seven habits. Today these habits are routine for me. Habits not only make a difference, they make all the difference.

If you have some unwanted aspects of life or events you didn't choose, remember you can choose your attitude, beliefs, and actions.

They tried to bury us. They didn't know we were seeds.

—Mexican Proverb

Ready? Let's Go!

The 7 Habits of a BraveHearted Woman

First, I'll give you the entire list of habits, then write a summary of each. Of course, I could write a book on these habits alone—many fabulous authors have done just that. But I'm giving you the essential points so you can start implementing these habits right away.

Habits:

1. She lives by design.

2. She sets goals for herself.

3. She practices positive self-talk.

4. She invests in herself.

5. She never stops learning.

6. She is grateful and lives generously.

7. She has a morning routine. (*Yes, I'm sneaking in 6 more habits!*)

   ◊   Pray and meditate

   ◊   Read

   ◊   Review goals

   ◊   Journal

   ◊   Exercise

   ◊   Listen to podcast

1. Live by Design not Default

Develop a life plan. You wouldn't build a home without a blueprint. If you did, you might end up with a toilet in your living room or the front door opening into your main bedroom. So why try to build a successful and fulfilling life without an intentional plan, a purposeful blueprint designed to move you toward goals and your desired outcomes? Your life is far more valuable than anything you can build, so don't try to *wing it* and expect greatness.

You're meant to partner with God to discern and design your life plan. Why leave to chance what you are called to control? Only you can decide the quality of life you want to live. You are responsible for your happiness and success. You're not helpless or without power, remember? We've already discussed your abilities in earlier chapters. Your identity as a brave woman says, "I can do this."

Designing your life means you're intentional every day with your plan. You don't live haphazardly and hope to wake up one day and find your dream-life. No. Setting intentions for your life takes thought, prayer, communion with God, and daily planning. Not to mention accountability, learning, and stretching. All things you can do, BraveHeart.

Tony Robbins said once, "We are cognitive misers." We don't like to use our energy for thinking. A bravehearted woman, however, does not accept mental laziness. She discerns what's in the circle of her control and goes after the life and results she wants. You alone can design your life through your:

◊ attitude

◊ actions

◊ effort

◊ focus

◊ habits

◊ commitment

◊ discipline

◊ mindsets

You have total control over all these areas.

Some believers think they're not supposed to make plans for their life. They glibly say, "if you want to make God laugh, tell him your plans." I understand what they mean when they say this because God is sovereign, and his ways are higher than our ways. I agree. But that does not mean we're excused from biblical planning and taking dominion over the earthy realm of our life. We are the stewards, the managers of the life God has given us. What successful manager do you know that says, "I have no plans to make this business successful. That's not my job."

Proverbs 16:3 says, "Share your plans with the LORD, and you will succeed" (CEV).

Socio-economist, Randall Bell says people who are consistent with planning and use tools such as calendars and to-do lists are about three times more likely to become millionaires than those who don't use a schedule. Successful people live by design, not default. (*I bet you want to buy a calendar now, don't you?*)

So, what do you want for your life?

What dreams rumble within you?

What relationships do you want? Where would you like to travel? What amount of income would you like to earn? What's the ideal weight you'd like to reach or maintain? Where would you like to live? What would you like to accomplish in the next decade?

I encourage you to become a lavish thinker—not miserly—connect with your heart and sincerely reflect on those questions. God has placed the desires you feel within you, and he expects you to cultivate them and the life he has given you. Trust him.

May he give you the desire of your heart and make all your plans succeed.

—Psalms 20:4

2. Set Specific Goals

Setting goals is the first step in turning the invisible into the visible.

—Tony Robbins

Once you have a clear vision and blueprint of the life you want to live, turn those dreams into reality by setting goals. Napoleon Hill, famous author of *Think and Grow Rich*, said it this way, "A goal is a dream with a deadline." That's good, isn't it? You have beautiful dreams inside you, and by establishing and writing goals, you take the ideas and dreams you hold in your head and put them in your hands. That's the power of proper goal setting. Successful people like you master the art.

A well-written goal is the vehicle that gets you to where you want to go.

Think of it; many people make resolutions and mistakenly call them goals. But once they declare their goals, most people never refer to them again. They forget all about what they said they wanted.

That's because most people keep their goals in their heads or scribble them in some obscure notebook and then hide it in their nightstand drawer. However, when your goals are out of sight, they're out of your mind, too.

I accidentally ran across this thread in a chat forum the other day. It caught my eye because the title of the thread was titled "My Big Dream." I found it humorous, but also, so unfortunately common. See if you can detect what made me clip this conversation and share it with you:

Girl 1 - *I'm asking here in hopes someone knows the answer...My course for today (and my extra credit for yesterday which I didn't finish because I didn't know the answer) is "Recommit to Your Big Picture." I can't remember exactly what my big vision is. I can't be the only one who has forgotten. Is there a place on the app to find this? I feel like I've searched everywhere.*

Girl 2 Answers - *I also didn't remember mine, so took that as an opportunity to reassess. It's okay if it changes over time. Though it is frustrating, like crap, what DID I say way back yonder? Props to the people who actually journaled and have something to reference.*

Girl 3 Adds - *Yeah. I took notes and journaled as I went along so I knew what mine was. But I made a new one before I went back and looked at it because as you said above an "opportunity to reassess." My second vision was a lot better than my first one.*

These sweet girls don't know their big vision for life.

But a bravehearted woman practices the habit of writing her goals and reviews them daily to remind herself of where she wants to go.

Research shows that people who write their goals have a 42 percent increase in the likelihood of accomplishing just what they have written. That's a whopping 42 percent.

Write your goals and describe them in vivid detail. Be specific about what you want and when you want to have it. Give your dream a deadline. Then, keep your goals alive by making them visible. Post them in places where you'll see them every day: on your mirror, near your bed, on your phone or computer screen, on the refrigerator, or in your daily journal. Because the brain sees in pictures, take time to find images that represent your goal. As you visualize your goals, you increase your desire to achieve them, elevate your inspiration and motivation for action, and give your brain focus and fortitude.

3. Practice Positive Self-Talk

You can't have million-dollar confidence with an impoverished vocabulary. And you can't feel much like a bravehearted woman with negative, self-deprecating words cascading out of your mouth, flowing back into your ears. It's impossible to feel good about yourself and live your best life if you don't have the self-esteem to reach for your dreams. You must develop the habit of positive self-talk.

Positive self-talk flows from a foundational belief in the woman God created you to be. So, yes, you must believe in yourself—your worth and ability—and nurture yourself with words and enriching affirmations that challenge, encourage, and cheer you on.

Even when your inner bully is scolding you for not being something enough. Rise and tell her to hush. Don't give that internal critic the microphone.

Research says your brain is like a supercomputer. You have more knowledge and capability than you can imagine. But did you know that your self-talk is the programmer of that super and complex computer? Well, it is!

Your brain eavesdrops on your self-talk and acts accordingly. Through positive self-talk, your brain learns to push you higher, give solution-oriented creativity, provide energy for your tasks, and train you to think like a winner and expect greatness.

That's good news.

The bad news? With no positive affirmations—or worse—negative speech, your brain learns to hold you back with limitations, fears, expectations of failure, and stories of why you can't succeed.

Inspire yourself with such beautiful words of life build your spirit. Learn to talk yourself off the edge when needed. Give yourself a pep-talk and take control over self-doubt and pessimism. These are the habits of a bravehearted woman who chooses not to believe or accept the scary, negative, doomsday narrative taking place in her own head. It's OK to feel your hurt, acknowledge your pain, and grieve what you must. Then declare out loud what God's Word says about you. "I can do everything through Christ, who gives me strength" (Philippians 4:13 NLT).

Remember that positive self-talk is an intrinsic part of a healthy mind.

—Dr. Asa Don Brown

4. Invest in Yourself

One hallmark of people who live their dreams and achieve remarkable accomplishments is that they invest in themselves. They say, "making an investment in myself is good and loving for me and you."

I agree. Brave women invest in themselves.

I've coached many women who suddenly develop a scarcity mindset over investing in themselves for personal growth. They feel selfish or fear they appear vain, having a grand sense of self-importance. As a result, they neglect their needs to their own peril, putting everyone else first. Eventually, these women feel unfulfilled and frustrated.

Since you're a woman reading this, I can guess—with almost 100% accuracy—you relate to what I'm saying. We women often feel guilty for thinking of our own needs as if it's some extravagant behavior on our part.

May I tell you something? Stop the guilt.

Invest in yourself.

I'll tell you what I explain to them. Investing in yourself is not self-ish. It's self-worth. God gave you a life to steward. Don't squander opportunities to improve and grow yourself and call it humility. Push yourself to experience all the bigness of the life you're meant to have.

Spend the time to make yourself a priority.

Spend money on your growth and development. Buy the books, attend the seminars, hire the trainer, find a coach, wear the nice mascara, and purchase the shoes.

Think about it. How would you invest in yourself if you weren't afraid?

Would you go back to school and get your education?

Buy a gym membership and hire a trainer?

Take a trip to explore other countries?

Purchase an online course in an area of your interest?

Take dancing lessons?

Learn a foreign language?

Start your own company?

It may feel counter-intuitive to prioritize and invest in yourself, but you'll serve the world better and with more joy and enthusiasm when you're filled up.

> *People are mistaken when they think chasing your dream*
> *is a selfish thing to do. As if perhaps being average is an*
> *act of humility. As if perhaps wasting the talents you were*
> *given is proof that you're a considerate individual. It's not.*
> —Jon Acuff [18]

5. Be a Life-long Learner

Years ago, a popular campaign slogan stated, "The mind is a terrible thing to waste." Yet so many people do. They waste the potential of their mind. They believe once they've completed their formal education, their days of learning are over. Far too many midlife women admit they feel they're done learning. They don't read books, acquire new skills, take classes to learn new subjects, study technology, or pursue personal growth. Not only is that a terrible waste of their future potential, but it leaves women with a drab and unfulfilled life. Where is the exhilaration of becoming, of chasing our passion, of growing our gifts, of stretching our minds and achieving our goals? God created us with an innate drive to explore, learn, and achieve.

Lifelong learners stay curious about themselves, what else they can accomplish, what goals they can reach, and how else they can use their life to serve. Lifelong learners remain curious about the world, global issues, other countries, cultures, and people. They stay informed about new advancements and changes in society. As a result, they're prepared to step into fresh opportunities when they come their way.

As a bravehearted woman, I encourage you to make it your habit to grow, learn, and constantly expand your horizon. Keep going with ongoing personal development and further education in whatever form feels fun and challenging. You can pursue anything you desire. Only you are responsible for the quality of your life, so don't just lay back and coast down the lazy river. You've got more in you, and until you take your last breath, make it your aim to stay vibrantly alive. As the famous Benjamin Franklin quote suggests, "Most people die at 25 but aren't buried until 75."

6. Live with Gratitude and Generosity

I have a small artwork piece in my office engraved with these words: "A grateful heart is a magnet for miracles." When I'm tempted to complain or become disgruntled, I remember I'm about to attract more to complain about, so I stop, adjust my mindset, and say, "Thank you, Lord. I'm grateful."

Gratitude and generosity cause your life to flourish because you reap what you sow. When you live with these two spiritual, positive forces in your life, you're setting yourself up for victory, since both gratitude and generosity break the spirit of scarcity and greed. I've tested the theory that we cannot out-give God, and I can testify that it is true. Generosity is also a magnet for miracles.

When you journey with gratitude and generosity, you change, and very often, so do your circumstances. You emerge stronger, better, wiser, and freer.

We've learned a lot about the power of gratitude in the last several years. Research shows numerous benefits from possessing a grateful spirit, including health, relationship, financial, and psychological improvements.

Develop the habit of saying thank you. Excel in gratitude and watch what happens. Give lavishly, knowing you are *sowing*. And whatever leaves your hand in sowing will never leave your life in reaping. Miracles will greet you on the path you travel.

Gratitude turns what we have into enough and more. It turns denial into acceptance, chaos into order, confusion into clarity...it makes sense of our past, brings peace for today, and creates a vision for tomorrow.

—Melody Beattie

7. Seize the Morning with a Daily Routine

A morning routine habit will change you and set you on a path to success like nothing else. What is it? Performing a powerful morning routine. Before discovering the "secret sauce" of this keystone habit, I spent my mornings sipping coffee, chatting on the phone, watching the morning news, and eventually reading a devotional before jumping into the shower. Although I listened to a motivational message every morning while getting ready for work, I missed out on the incredible, science-backed benefits of a specific morning routine. Once I started my journey of personal growth and development early in 2000, I learned first-hand how a morning routine changes everything.

Author, speaker, and success coach, Terri Savelle Foy, says her morning routine changed her life. She explains how she went from living an unorganized, unsuccessful, and undisciplined life to becoming the founder and CEO of a thriving international ministry organization, writing numerous books, speaking worldwide, and having her own TV show. And what one thing do you think she accredits her success to? You guessed it—her morning routine.

The most successful people in the world have specific habits and rituals that have led them to success. In my life, my morning routine and daily discipline have led me to where I am today. When people ask me, "How did your life change so drastically?" I say, "I changed my routine, and it changed my life.[19]

A daily morning routine will set you apart, just like it has for countless other fulfilled and successful people, and it's the best time of the day to start your success habits. When you wake up early to seize the morning, you take dominion over your entire day while positioning yourself for incredible growth and development.

Morning time is an uncontested, quiet, and tranquil time to think, create, meditate, and pray. While the world sleeps, you're elevating.

Your willpower is at its highest in the morning, giving you an extra boost in focus and determination. As a result, you can get the most important stuff done before 8 AM.

You set a positive tone for the rest of your day. You keep stress at bay when you take control of your day.

Robin Sharma, leadership expert, and author of *The 5 AM Club: Own Your Morning. Elevate Your Life*, is a radical believer in owning the mornings. He says, "Take excellent care of the front end of your day, and the rest of your day will pretty much take care of itself. Own your morning. Elevate your life."

When you own the mornings, you elevate your spiritual, psychological, emotional, physical, and financial life. Every aspect of you is impacted and improved.

Are you ready to elevate?

Then it's time to conquer your mornings. Setting the alarm clock just 30 minutes early gives you the first win. And, if you win your morning, you win your day. When you win your days, you win your weeks and months. When you win your months, you consistently and successfully win in your private and public life. Remember, what you practice in private is rewarded in public.

How to Start a Morning Routine

Before we think about the time of day, whether to start at 4:00 AM, 5:00 AM, or 6:00 AM, let's establish that everyone has a morning. Unless you get swept away during the night, you will wake up. But what happens next is what sets leaders, winners, high-achievers, and you apart. You wake up on purpose, with purpose, and seize the day.

Determine when you need to be ready to face the world and give yourself the extra time you want for your morning routine.

I've discovered the best time to start my morning ritual is at 6:06 AM. I call it the "6:06 Rise: 6 Habits at 6 AM." (I often wake much earlier, but my routine will begin at 6:06.)

At that time, my world is still quiet and undemanding. I cherish a few moments sitting in the stillness.

Decide what key practices you want to include in your morning routine.

I practice 6 habits that help me feel my best and prepare me for the day ahead. I share these to give you an idea of how a morning routine can look. The key here is to find what works for you.

Prayer and Meditation

First, I greet God: God the Father, Son, and Holy Spirit. I invite him into my day and ask him to fill me afresh. Then I pray and meditate on His Word while also practicing diaphragmatic breathing. Since I used to be plagued with anxiety, this physical practice of meditative breathing keeps me balanced.

Reading

My reading begins with my Bible, highlighting scriptures that speak to me. Then I read a book on business growth and development or about a subject I want to learn.

Journaling

Journaling comes next. My journal is much more than writing about how I feel and what I'm thinking. I do that—but the journal I designed leads me through a series of tabs that each represent a purpose and intention for me. My tabs include

Gratitude

Goals-Long-Term and Short-Term

Capture and Schedule

My Intentions

Daily Affirmations

Creative Ideas

Classic Journaling

I write what God speaks to me, ideas and inspirations I receive, scriptures I'm meditating on, my emotional and physical states, and more. This is my favorite practice and how I stay connected to what's happening in and around me.

Exercise

I move my body every day. I love exercise … when it's over. To keep me accountable, I head to the gym with my husband three days a week, and the other days I work out from home, walk, or stretch. When I've completed my exercise for the day, I feel supercharged, and I'm sure my self-esteem gets a significant boost too. I feel fabulous. Exercise is a serious habit to install in your routine, especially as you age. If you rest, you rust.

Listen to Learning Podcasts

I take in content every day. Whether it's motivational, coaching, training, or learning, I listen to faith-building messages daily. It's easy to incorporate into your morning. Just start a podcast or audiobook while exercising, getting ready, doing your hair, or putting on your make-up. I learn something new each day, and I enjoy being challenged so I can grow.

> **For Dawn's Daily Journal Visit**
>
> https://www.braveheartedwoman.com/resources

Review Goals

Most of us agree setting goals is vital. Unless we revisit those goals, it's unlikely we will accomplish them. I make it my habit to review my goals every day. This way, I stay on track with the dreams I have said are significant to me. It's important I do something every day which moves me toward reaching my goal. Reviewing what I want and why I want it keeps me forward-focused and fuels my determination.

These are my rituals. I've heard other morning warriors also practice these habits:

◊ Map out the day

◊ Create a daily to-do list

◊ Eat a healthy breakfast

◊ Take a cold shower

◊ Walk in nature

◊ Stretch

◊ Drink a glass of water

◊ Write

◊ Prayer walk

◊ Practice visualization

If you don't make the time to work on creating the life you want, you're eventually going to be forced to spend a lot of time dealing with a life you don't want.

—Kevin Ngo, Motivational Coach

Start with one or two elements and become consistent.

I'll repeat it; just start. Don't overwhelm yourself with too much, too soon. One habit done well is worth more than six habits not done. It has taken time and consistency for me to create a routine that works for me. But I can promise no matter how you start, once you discover the life-transformative power of routine, you won't want to quit.

Increase your routine as you go

Once you conquer your small routine, try to set the alarm another 30 minutes earlier and make the additions you desire. Include exercise at this point if you haven't already.

These habits are the best practices you can incorporate into your day, creating a joyful lifestyle designed to maximize your time on earth. The only question is whether we have the discipline to follow through. In the next chapter, I will help you harness the power of self-discipline you'll need to follow through on these brave habits.

Rise before the sun. There is a reason why the great men and women of history, movement makers, great thinkers and philosophers rose before the sun; there is a magic in the air at 5 AM. It's the time of greatest quietude and tranquility. … you've got the world to yourself!

—Robin Sharma

Brave Challenge #10: Plan

Develop a morning routine. What time will you rise? What elements will you include? Remember to start small and increase as you overpower the pillow!

Design Your Brave Life Plan

If you don't design your own life plan, chances are you'll fall into someone else's plan. And guess what they have planned for you? Not much.

—Jim Rohn

Congratulations. You've read this far, and that tells me you're serious about becoming a bravehearted woman who is living her life full out. Well done. Now it's time to pull together everything we've discussed and assemble your ultimate Brave Life Plan.

Having a blueprint of where I'm headed reduces stress and anxiety about life. I have a clear desired destination and a strategic plan to get there. And because I'm focused on what I want, decision-making is more effortless. I know what opportunities to say yes to and what ventures to decline.

So, now it's your turn. If you haven't done it yet, this is the time to design your Brave Life Plan.

The following steps will guide you as you develop your plan.

Clearly Define What You Want

In 2008, after my divorce, my life was wiped clean. The future looked bleak and barren. I didn't know what to do, where to go, or how to earn a living. I was terrified. But as I reflect on that difficult trial, I can undeniably testify God was with me every second. He had not forgotten me, nor was he without a plan for me. God was already ahead of me in my future, wooing me into new territory. I prayed my spiritual eyes would open to see a fresh vision.

I started with prayer and a yellow legal pad. Although dreaming came slowly at first, eventually, my soul awakened. I grew eager about the possibilities that awaited me. A renewed vision faintly appeared on the horizon, growing ever brighter.

Regardless of where you're starting, whether from a place of trial and difficulty or merely a fresh chapter unfolding for you, your future is directly linked to the clarity of vision you hold for yourself.

What is your big picture *vision*? What can you see for yourself? What would you like to be different in your life? What do you truly want? Remember, your vision is a picture of life's coming attractions and is unique to you. The image you hold in your heart reveals the answer to the "why" of your life; *Why am I here? What gives me meaning?* Bravely write the dreams you have here. Dream big.

____

____

____

Go after your dream no matter how unattainable others
think it is.
—John Assaraf

Practice the 5 Fortitudes

The 5 Fortitudes are the supportive framework that will propel you toward achieving your Brave Life Plan.

Here's a review: Remember our acronym B.R.A.V.E. to help you.

Fortitude 1. **B**old Vision

What do you see? (*How many times is she going to say this?!*)

To reach your vision, you need to believe, without a doubt, two essentials:

◊ God is for you.

◊ You are worthy of living the life you dream of.

Fortitude 2. **R**eal Identity

Believing the two basic truths takes identity confidence. Fortitude Two builds an unstoppable identity whose foundation is the Lord. As you grow in confidence, you become who you want to be, ready to risk greater steps of faith to accomplish your goals and dreams. You may need more marble chipped away to unleash the angel held within, but you're on your way to accepting the truth about you!

I saw the angel in the marble and carved until I set (her) free.
—Michelangelo

Fortitude 3. **A**ble Mindsets.

Reaching your vision takes positive, well-guarded, resilient mindsets. You focus on what is right, true, honorable, and excellent. You press on toward the goal because grit and gratitude keep you from giving up in despair. As Winston Churchill said, "Success is the ability to go from failure to failure without losing enthusiasm."

Fortitude 4. **V**irtuous Talk.

The words of a bravehearted woman inspire all who hear her. You undergird your vision by speaking words of life. You declare victory over yourself and over God's plan for your life. Words of doubt and defeat don't flow from your mouth. Terri Savelle Foy once said that you can train yourself to speak words of life by adding this phrase to the end of each statement, "just as I want it to be." *Gulp.!* You'll think twice before you utter mindless words.

Fortitude 5. **E**xcellent Action

Finally, you're not just talk; you put action to your story. The habits I've outlined for you will transform you. But not if you only read about them. Not even if you agree and accept the truth about them. Fortitude five says you must ACT on them. Do the work and get the reward. It's that simple. You are brave. You take courageous action toward your goals.

Of the 5 Fortitudes, which one presents the biggest challenge for you?

____

____

____

Be aware of your potential areas of weakness, so you can fortify yourself when determination and desire wane.

Prioritize and Set Your Goals.

Your ultimate brave life design will be broken down into small, bite-sized goals. Don't tackle everything at once. When you're ready to take action toward your vision, determine your priorities. What goal do you want to accomplish first? Focus on your top three goals and let the rest unfold.

Just remember to surrender the *how* to God. You don't need to know how your brave vision will come to pass. Just trust that it will.

You'll soon discover that reaching your aspirations raises your self-esteem and increases your faith in believing God for big things. Once my vision was clear, I started accomplishing goals that seemed impossible in my previous life. Today, I reach for the moon because I realize so much more is available and obtainable than my former mindset allowed me to consider. So, you, too, will be astonished at what you're capable of when you believe God for your dreams.

What are your top three goals for the next year?

1. ____

2. ____

3. ____

Shoot for the moon. Even if you miss, you'll land among the stars.

—Les Brown

Push With Your Why

If you want to consistently advance with ample amounts of passion and energy and incrementally achieve the ambitions included in your brave life design, you need to make sure your design only consists of the goals you care deeply about. That may seem obvious, but you'd be surprised how many people design the life of someone else's dreams. There's little evidence that people reach goals when they're not deeply connected to the reason they want it. If you're only somewhat interested or committed, you'll lack the juice to follow through with the discipline it requires to reach your destination. Clearly articulating *why,* you want this future puts fuel in your tank. When others would quit, you'll keep on pressing, pushing, and fighting for your dreams. When persuasive justifications and rationalizations arise, your *why* will tap on your heart's door to remind you of your bigger picture. With a compelling *why,* you'll recharge, but without it, you'll most likely wave the white flag.

For each goal you determine you want to achieve, write *why* you want to accomplish this.

Consider:

How will your life improve? How will the lives of those you love improve? What will you gain if you reach this goal, and what will you lose if you don't? What will it cost you if you miss this opportunity?

____

____

____

____

Plan and Do the Work

Once you have your strategic plan, executing is the only thing left. It's *Go Time.* Make it your commitment to do something every day to bring you closer to achieving your goal. If you lack motivation, keep picturing the finished product, reminding yourself how awesome it will be when you arrive at your destiny.

If it's self-discipline you lack, then consider making yourself accountable to a coach, partner, or friend, but honestly, if you can't make yourself obey yourself to go after your vision, then I think you may need a new goal. As the late Myles Munroe said, "Find a vision so compelling it imposes self-discipline on you." The key to a vibrant life is to find such an irresistible vision that self-discipline easily happens. Otherwise, if you lack self-discipline, you're headed for a future of frustration, failure, and unfulfillment. You must learn to make yourself obey yourself.

The Value of Self-Discipline

In his book, *No Excuses: The Power of Discipline*, Brian Tracy shares a story about a chance encounter with success and achievement legend Kop Kopmeyer. Kop had written four bestselling books, each containing over 250 success principles Kop had derived from more than 50 years of research and study. Brain Tracy asked Kop what so many others have asked, "Of all the thousands of success principles you have discovered, which do you think is the most important?" Brian said Kop smiled at him with a twinkle in his eye, as if he had been asked this question many times, and replied without hesitating, "The most successful principle of all was stated by Elbert Hubbard, one of the most prolific writers in American history, at the beginning of the twentieth century who said, 'Self-discipline is the ability to do what you should do when you should do it, whether or not you feel like it or not.'

Then Kop said, "There are 999 other success principles I have found in my reading and experience, but without self-discipline, none of them work. With self-discipline, they all work." Brian ended the story by saying, "Self-discipline is the key to personal greatness."[20]

Self-discipline is the grit that makes you unstoppable. But without it, you'll never rise to the greatness you've been created for.

You may have great dreams and big goals, but *winners and losers have the same goals*, so it's not the goal that determines an individual's success—it's the discipline. Do you take consistent action toward those goals? That's what makes the difference.

I've met plenty of talented people who've squandered their gifts because they can't organize their life or discipline their actions. That's sad for them and for the whole world, who would benefit from their unique offering.

One gifted woman I know recently told me, "I don't like the word routine. It feels so rigid. I prefer to flow." And flow she did, right into obscurity.

God's Word teaches when there is no vision, people abandon restraints and run wild. They don't want the pain of self-discipline. But can I tell you something? They're headed for a pain much greater—the pain of regret.

You have to detest mediocrity in your life.

Just like Tom did.

Tom's Story

Tom Bilyeu is a popular podcasting host and entrepreneur.

But he didn't start out that way.

Tom was a self-described lazy, chubby, and insecure child. His first job was delivering newspapers, yet he was so scared to knock on doors he couldn't collect his paycheck. He cheated his way through school and hated every second. Tom battled massive anxiety. Even his mother assumed he wouldn't go far in life. He showed no signs of success.

Still, his mom pushed him off to college, despite her belief that he would fail. Once at college, Tom studied film, but a new interest bubbled up. Because he grew up in an obese family, watching family members eat themselves to death, Tom developed a passion for health and fitness. While at school, he shed 60 pounds.

Tom Bilyeu's weight-loss success and his family history sparked a passion for health and fitness, so he developed a company to create a healthy snack. Tom wanted his company to be based on work that would make him happy and provide value for others. So, Tom and his wife, Lisa, started making healthy nutrition bars out of their kitchen. After a few months, they perfected the recipe with no added sugar and great taste.

Finally, their product was launched. Tom sent a thousand hand-written letters and a sample of his nutritional bar to fitness influencers everywhere. Before he knew it, Quest Nutrition was born, and Tom was soon the founder of a company worth over $1 billion.

Tom says the secret to his success was his mindset. He grew up as a lazy child but dedicated himself to changing his habits and nurturing a growth mindset.

Next, Tom established a strict morning routine, including a workout and meditation. He firmly believes all successful people have a morning routine.

Tom also started goal setting, effectively using his time and taking action toward his goals. He says although he used to lay in bed for 5 to 6 hours a day, he now has a vision that wakes him up and gets him out of bed. Rising early is a discipline he has cultivated.

Today, Tom coaches others on changing their lives and says the secret is discipline. "Once you have iron-clad discipline, you're no longer a slave to your lesser impulses. That's why discipline is so critical."

Tom went from unmotivated to mover and shaker, not just because he tapped his passion and vision but because he learned to harness self-discipline.

That's what I want for you. Go from where you are now to where you want to be—from pain to purpose, mundane to magnificent, faint-hearted to bravehearted. And all you have to do is commit to the discipline of becoming 1% better today than you were yesterday.

That's it!

Just 1%. You can do it.

1% Better

If you can get 1% better each day for one year, following the rules of compound interest, you'll end up 37.78 times better than you were last year.

What would a 37% improvement in your health look like for you? How about your finances? Your personal growth or relationships? You don't have to take daily quantum leaps to change your life. Transformation happens in the slow and methodical daily, not the spectacular "once-in-awhile." Just discipline yourself to take one small step every day.

But you may say, "Dawn, sometimes I get uninspired or tired of pursuing my goals. My routine feels unexciting." I hear you. Sometimes we even battle discouragement because we don't see results fast enough. But that's why we need discipline. When motivation doesn't show up—and most often, it doesn't—our discipline keeps us on track. I'd rather have the pain of doing the hard stuff than the pain of regretting missed opportunities.

It's only when looking back 2, 5, or 10 years later that the value of good habits and the cost of bad ones become strikingly apparent.

—James Clear

1% better can happen with just 15 minutes a day.

- ◊ 15 minutes a day for one week equals 105 minutes or 1.75 hours.

- ◊ 15 minutes a day for 30 days equals 450 minutes or 7.5 hours.

- ◊ 15 minutes a day for 365 days equals 5,475 minutes or 91.25 hours.

How would 91. 25 hours of push-ups, jumping jacks, and walking change your health?

How would 91.25 hours of reading, praying, meditating, and journaling change your heart and mind?

How would 91.25 hours of studying, writing, and planning change your career and financial picture?

Just think of where you could be one year from now if you applied the 1% better rule. What would happen for you if you chose 4 areas of daily improvement, each with a 15-minute block. With just one hour a day, you could reach fitness, financial, spiritual, and personal development goals.

What four areas would you like to improve?

1.

2.

3.

4.

The smallest of implementations is always worth more
than the grandest of intentions.

—Robin Sharma

Shiny Object Syndrome

Terri Savelle calls it the *Popcorn Effect.*

Debbie Ford calls it the *No Cookie Zone*

Sandford University calls it *The Marshmallow Test.*

I call it the *Shiny Object Syndrome.*

Whatever we call it, the principle is the same. It's the inability to delay gratification and exert self-discipline.

Research shows that most people give up their long-term desire for a short-term, shiny object win. (If you can call it a win at all.) Undisciplined people want instant gratification. Yet the ability to delay pleasure is proven to be one of the most critical success characteristics of life.

Sure, we all give ourselves permission to have a day off once in a while. I think that's healthy, especially when we make that choice in advance and with a plan of when and how we will get back on the path.

Most people, however, don't premeditate their day off. Instead, they habitually cave in under the pressure of the *right here and now*—they want what they want when they want it. But regularly choosing to give in to popcorn, cookies, marshmallows, or shiny objects, is ultimately a choice to forfeit dreams and settle for the mundane.

That's what most people do.

They have lived their lifetime choosing average over exquisite and instant gratification over long-term destiny.

The Marshmallow Test

During the 1960s, psychologist Walter Mischel conducted what is now famously known as "The Marshmallow Test," an experiment designed to explore the ability of children to delay gratification and exert self-control in the face of temptation. The study involved children aged 3-5 in the preschool at Stanford University. Each child was given one delicious fluffy marshmallow and told they could eat it immediately or wait for a while and receive two delicious marshmallows.

Once the researcher left, some kids just couldn't wait. They immediately devoured the marshmallow.

The rest mustered the willpower to resist eating it but employed various techniques to help. I've seen multiple videos of this same experiment by parents, and it's hilarious to see what children do to resist the temptation to eat the marshmallow. The kids in the research study covered their eyes, turned away from the marshmallow, talked to themselves, sang songs, wiggled, squirmed, and bounced in their chairs. Some even tried to sleep to control their impulses and earn the reward.

Twelve to fourteen years later, Mischel and his colleagues followed up with the participants and found something astonishing. The kids who could control their impulses and delay gratification had better life outcomes, starting with higher SAT scores of a staggering 210 points. They also were more successful in business, relationships, and self-confidence. They outdid their instant marshmallow-eating friends in their ability to control stress and manage their personal life.

I want to think that the lesson here is obvious—eat more marshmallows! But, no, the real lesson here is self-discipline and the ability to defer gratification for something better is the bedrock of success.

How about you? Do you struggle to choose discipline over delights, self-control over snacks, or education over entertainment?

What area of weakness do you want to improve?

Is it watching television over reading a faith-building book?

Or are you tempted to eat treats and goodies over sticking to your healthy meal plan?

Maybe your battle zone is shopping and spending over saving and planning?

Whatever it is for you, stop choosing average over exquisite, end self-sabotage, and harness self-control. If you invest in long-term goals instead of short-term goodies, you will have the abundant life Jesus promised.

When you take control of your habits, you take control of your life.

—Terri Savelle

Final Thoughts

Remember you are a masterpiece. God created you, gifted you, and has a purpose for you.

He is the ultimate Author of your life, and you, dear BraveHeart, are co-author. Your life is meant to be a page-turner, so don't settle for a life of existence rather than significance. Live your dream.

Next, apply the principles you've learned in this book. They are biblical and will change your life.

Love yourself and fight for your dreams. Live on purpose and by design. Invest in yourself because you're worth it.

Finally, embrace your grit and shine your glitter! Show the world that you are a BraveHearted Woman here to live in all the joy, abundance, and fulfillment Jesus came to give.

Brave Challenge #11: Complete

Finish well. Complete all the challenges and you'll be well on your way to a brave life.

Brave Challenge #1: Engage

Brave Challenge #2: Shed

Brave Challenge #3: Rise

Brave Challenge #4: Commit

Brave Challenge #5: Dream

Brave Challenge #6: Sculpt

Brave Challenge #7: Choose

Brave Challenge #8: Listen

Brave Challenge #9: Action

Brave Challenge #10: Plan

Brave Challenge #11: Complete

For more help visit me at

https://www.braveheartedwoman.com/contact-me

The BraveHearted Womanfesto

I am a woman of passion and purpose.

I am worthy of love and happiness.

I am brave. I don't let fear stop me from possessing my dreams.

I show love for myself.

I am confident to use my voice.

I set and respect healthy boundaries.

I am in charge of my happiness.

I am healthy.

I face challenges head on.

I don't feel guilty when I choose to put my needs first.

I boldly say I am beautiful, intelligent, powerful, enough.

I am grateful.

I learn from failure and rebound quickly. I am thankful for the opportunity to grow.

I am my best friend.

I can.

A BRAVEHEARTED FIGHT

No one will fight for your dreams but you.

A bravehearted women learns to fight.

> We fight to create a vision for our life. And we fight to keep that vision alive.
>
> We fight for our ideas.
>
> We fight to keep our mind focused in the right direction.
>
> We fight our inner critic and negative feelings about ourselves.
>
> We fight off self-limitations and sabotage.
>
> We fight off fears, procrastination, and laziness.
>
> We fight to reach goals and manifest our dreams. We refuse the comfort zone.
>
> We fight against opposition and obstructions, interruptions, and disruption.
>
> We fight for progress and productivity.
>
> Our fight is the manifestation of our confidence.

Bravehearted women have developed a belief in themselves that says,

> *My dream is worthy. My potential shall be tapped and pursued.*
>
> *I am a worthy goal, who has worthy goals. My dreams are valuable."*

Meet the Author

Dawn Damon is an influencer, global communicator, podcaster, high-performance coach, and best-selling author.

Her 5 award-winning books, include *When a Woman You Love Was Abused*, published by Kregel Publications, *When the Woman Abused Was Me*, *The Freedom Challenge: 60 Days to Untie the Cords that Bind You*, Redemption Press, and most recently the Amazon Best-Selling Book *The Freedom Challenge for Men: 60 Days to Untie the Cords that Bind You.*

Dawn is the founder and CEO of New Dawn Rising and the BraveHearted Woman, an enterprise and a non-profit designed to cultivate the vision of women dreamers, and equip them to live their best life.

Dawn, is also known as "The BraveHeart Mentor" hosts a podcast called the *BraveHearted Woman*—a program that calls out the vision of women who want to reach for their BRAVE.

As a popular keynote and conference speaker, Dawn is an engaging and dynamic; a communicator who inspires her audiences to maximize their divine purpose and potential.

As one client put it, "Dawn ignites my dreams!" Through coaching, teaching, story-telling, and splashes of humor, she awakens the gifts and callings in every person.

Dawn has an extensive history of Radio and Television. She serves as an authority on sexual abuse and trauma, and a regularly featured contributor to Salem Radio's *Life!Line* with Craig Roberts San Francisco drive time talk show, featured in the nation's 4th largest radio market.

Throughout Dawn's career, she has continually pushed the limits, believing God for big, big things. She worked closely with New York bestselling author Cecil Murphey, co-author of 90 Minutes in Heaven and When A Man You Love Was Abused. Together, Dawn and Cecil presented two conferences titled, When Someone You Love was Abused: Help for Those Suffering from Childhood Traumas.

In 2014 Dawn and her husband Paul planted a multi-cultural Church called Tribes located in the North Grand Rapids area, where she was the lead Pastor for 7 years.

Dawn and her husband Paul Damon reside in the Grand Rapids, MI area and have a full family of three married children, two college-age sons, and eleven grandchildren.

Acknowledgments

Thank you, Paul for your endless love and support. You make me brave. With your encouragement, I've taken leaps of faith to become the woman God destined for me. I love you.

Thank you, Bonnie for tireless hours of dedication and selfless giving. Your pursuit of excellence is a true blessing. You're a remarkable gift and a sparkling gem. I love you dearly.

Bible Versions

Unless otherwise marked Scripture quotations marked are taken from the Holy Bible, New International Version®, NIV®. Copyright © 1973, 1978, 1984, 2011 by Biblica, Inc.™ Used by permission of Zondervan. All rights reserved worldwide. www.zondervan.com The "NIV" and "New International Version" are trademarks registered in the United States Patent and Trademark Office by Biblica, Inc.™

Scripture quotations marked NKJV are taken from the New King James Version®. Copyright © 1982 by Thomas Nelson, Inc. Used by permission. All rights reserved.

Scripture quotations marked AMP are taken from the Amplified® Bible, Copyright © 1954, 1958, 1962, 1964, 1965, 1987 by The Lockman Foundation

Used by permission." (www.Lockman.org)

Scripture quotations marked "KJV" are taken from the Holy Bible, King James Version, Cambridge, 1769.

Scripture quotations marked THE MESSAGE are taken from THE MESSAGE, copyright© by Eugene H. Peterson 1993, 1994, 1995, 1996, 2000, 2001, 2002. Used by permission of NavPress Publishing Group.

Scripture quotations marked NLT are taken from the Holy Bible, New Living Translation, copyright ©1996, 2004, 2007 by Tyndale House Foundation. Used by permission of Tyndale House Publishers, Inc., Carol Stream, Illinois 60188. All rights reserved.

Scripture quotations marked HCSB are taken from the Holman Christian Standard Bible®, Copyright © 1999, 2000, 2002, 2003, 2009 by Holman Bible Publishers. Used by permission. Holman Christian Standard Bible®, Holman CSB®, and HCSB® are federally registered trademarks of Holman Bible Publishers.

Scripture quotations marked (CEV) are from the Contemporary English Version Copyright © 1991, 1992, 1995 by American Bible Society, Used by Permission.

Scripture quotations marked TPT are from The Passion Translation®. Copyright © 2017, 2018 by Passion & Fire Ministries, Inc. Used by permission. All rights reserved. ThePassionTranslation.com.

Endnotes

1	Peter Scazzero, *Emotionally Healthy Spirituality: It's Impossible to Be Spiritually Mature, While Remaining Emotionally Immature*, Zondervan; Updated edition, April 25, 2017

2	https://www.thehealthy.com/mental-health/what-makes-people-brave/

3	Richelle Goodrich, *Smile Anyway: Quotes, Verse, and Grumblings for Every Day of the Year*, 2015

4	Brene' Brown, *Rising Strong: How the Ability to Reset Transforms the Way We Live, Love, Parent, and Lead,* Random House Publishing Group, 2017

5	Peter Scazzero, *Emotionally Healthy Spirituality: It's Impossible to be Spiritually Mature While Remaining Emotionally Immature,* Zondervan, 2014

6	Ari Zoland, *Tony Robbins Says This 4-Letter Word Is the Greatest Obstacle in Pursuing Your Dreams,* December 26, 2017

7	Nick Broomfieldand Rudi Dolezal, *Whitney: Can I Be Me?,* Documentary, 2017

8	IBID

9	Bronnie Ware, *The Top Five Regrets of the Dying: A Life Transformed by the Dearly Departing,* Hay House Inc., Reprint Edition 2012

10	Rachel Hollis, *Girl Stop Apologizing: A Shame Free Plan for Embracing and Achieving Your Goals,* Harper Collins, 2019

11	Steven Spielberg, *Hook,* Film, 1991

12	Soren Kierkegaard, *The Master Thief,* Journal 1 A 11-16, September 12, 1835

13   Peter Scazzero, *Emotionally Healthy Spirituality: It's Impossible to be Spiritually Mature While Remaining Emotionally Immature,* Zondervan, 2014

14   (Acuff, Quitter: Closing the Gap Between Your Day Job and Your Dream Job, 2011)

15   Angela Duckworth, Grit: The Power and Passion of Perseverance, Scribner, 2016

16   Adapted from Tony Robbins, https://www.tonyrobbins.com/mind-meaning/whats-your-morning-ritual/

17   Rachel Hollis, *Girl Stop Apologizing: A Shame Free Plan for Embracing and Achieving Your Goals*, Harper Collins, 2019

18   Jon Acuff, *Start: Punch Fear in the Face, Escape Average and Do Work that Matters*, Ramsey Press, 2013

19   Terri Savelle Foy, *Mind Over Mattress*, https://www.cfaith.com/index.php/article-display/22-articles/christian-living/27838-mind-over-mattress-the-routine

20   Brian Tracy, *No Excuses! The Power of Self-Discipline*, Vanguard Press, 2012

Made in United States
Orlando, FL
08 November 2023

38710285R10107